GALWAY TR...

2024

The Ultimate Travel Guide to IRELAND GALWAY -
Top Things to do, Best Places to Visit, Hidden Gems,
Travel Budget, Tips and Tricks

NOMAD NICK

CONTENTS

Poulnabrone Portal Tomb (Poulnabrone dolmen)

INTRODUCTION

Galway is a big county with a lot of great places to see and things to do. Galway City is known all over the world as a shopping, culture, and nightlife paradise. It's usually the first-place tourists go because it's easy to get to from the rest of the country by road and rail. When you come here, you'll be taken in by its charm, easy going vibe, and nice people. Walk around the city's small, cobblestone streets and enjoy its cafes, shops, and gourmet restaurants. At night, the city comes to life with pulsing parties and bars and the sound of Irish traditional music that stays in the air, so just follow the sounds.

Galway is a city that has something to offer everyone. Whether you're interested in history, culture, food, or nightlife, you're sure to find something to your liking in Galway.

If you want to learn more about Galway or need a guide to help you plan your trip, please continue reading this book. I've included everything you need to know about Galway, from its history and attractions to its food, nightlife and many more. I've also provided number of days itineraries for different types of travellers, so you can plan the perfect trip for your needs.

Let's go on adventure with NOMAD NICK!

15 Gorgeous Reasons to Visit GALWAY in 2024

Hooker Galway

Ireland's craft beer scene is growing quickly, but Galway Hooker, named after a local type of boat, was one of the first and is still one of the best. It tastes like a complex pale ale. Two brothers started making the brew in Oranmore, just outside of the town, in 2006. It is now almost as common in the town as the famous black stuff from Dublin, which is just down the road.

Cathedral of Galway

Galway Cathedral was built in the 1960s, which is a long way from the old churches that line the streets of Ireland. It has an unusual relic in a painting of John F. Kennedy. The strange mix of architectural styles will be interesting to people who like buildings, but for others, it's just a stark, reverent, and slightly bleak sign of the city.

The Museum Of The Claddagh Ring

The Claddagh Ring Museum is devoted to what might be Galway's most important cultural sign. It tells the story of the romantic jewelry of the Callagh district over hundreds of years. The rings, which have two hearts and a crown, can be a sign of availability or a love bond.

As well as giving information about the ring itself, the museum's many artifacts give a lot of information about the history of the area.

The Rugby Team Connacht

Connacht has always been the weakest of the four Irish provincial rugby clubs, which all play in the same league with teams from Scotland and Wales. However, their recent success has turned them into a team that plays attractive and successful rugby. The (relatively) small Galway Sportsgrounds is where they play, so you can get right up close to the roaring action.

Quay Street.

Galway's main shopping street, Shop Street, is probably one of the most beautiful streets in Ireland. It is a pedestrian-only walk that is always full of buskers and street artists. If you want to eat, go to Quay Street. The pubs invite you in, and the shops' bright, charming fronts and window displays make you want to go inside. It's still shopping, but it has music, is calmer, and looks much better.

Kai

Kai is a simple but very high-end restaurant that is committed to ethical supply and organic food. One of the best things about it is that it changes with the seasons, so it's hard to know what you might eat before you go there. You must stop at a cafe on Sea Road during the day. For dinner, you'll probably need to make a reservation at this famous spot. Check out the seafood places in the area as well.

The Heart of Wood

The Wooden Heart is a toy store that looks like it was taken right out of the middle of the last century. It sells dolls, hand-carved wooden toys, and imaginative, exciting things for kids to play with. It doesn't hurt anyone and is probably the most beautiful old building on Quay Street, where you can often find a busker sitting right outside its perfectly arranged window to play music while you look through the stuff.

The Salthill Promenade

Salthill Promenade is a long stretch of seaside path with posh hotels and penny arcades. It is the part of the city that has given in to a charming, throwback kind of localized tourism. It has great views of Galway Bay and is a great place to go for a walk. If you see the diving platform against the setting sun, you might be tempted to jump into the cold Atlantic.

The Food Market

Church Lane's local food market has been around for hundreds of years. It started small, with just bread, fruit, and veggies, but it has grown to become a great place to grab a quick bite or try local (and not-so-local) treats. The best time to visit the tented corner is on Saturdays (hours vary based on when you go) when people shopping for breakfast mix with local artists and tourists.

The Roisin Dubh

People say that Roisin Dubh is one of the best pubs in Ireland. It's both a pub and a live music venue, and local hero Gugai picks the music. It's a great place for artsy people in Galway to meet up. Almost every night of the week, something is going on, and some of the best bands in Ireland play here often. But even when there's not much going on musically, this place is a huge social hub that's almost always full of excited locals. The whole street is sometimes turned into a "silent disco." Let's face it: being known as one of the best places in Ireland to drink beer is no small task.

Cruises on the Corrib River

The Corrib is a calm river until it hits the shore of Galway City, but a cruise along its waters is a great way to see the buildings and wildlife and get a feel for the city's outskirts. Most boats take you to Lake Corrib, which is Ireland's biggest lake. Even though some of the nighttime tours don't have many things to see, they do have a DJ and a lively bar, which makes for a different kind of night out.

Festival of oysters in Galway

An event that celebrates Atlantic fish is held every year in September and is a big part of Galway's culture. The oyster festival has some big events, like the world championship for breaking oysters, the parade, and the dinner and ball, but what's most special is how it affects the city as a whole. Take bars, which often serve a small plate of oysters with certain pints, which are, of course, made to go with seafood. Start digging.

Charlie Byrne's Bookstore

Charlie Byrne's is a Galway institution. It is the kind of (mostly used) bookstore that book lovers could spend hours looking through. They say that they always have more than 100,000 books in stock, which are stored on long shelves and full tables. If that's not enough, they open a motherload at the warehouse every Saturday.

Kayak journeys

Outdoors Ireland is the main company that offers kayak trips in Galway, which is a great place for the sport because it has almost every kind you can think of. For pros, there's surfing the splashing waves of the lock in front of a crowd of people sitting by the Spanish Arch and watching with rapt attention. For newbies, there is the calm Lough Corrib, and sea kayaking (depending on the weather) is a good middle ground. On trips out to Mutton Island, seals and sometimes killer whales can be seen.

Spanish Arch

The Spanish Arch was built in the 16th century. It is made up of two large gates made of thick local stone. In recent years, the area has become known as "Buckfast Plaza" as a joke. The name comes from the fact that locals like to drink an extremely messy tonic wine there instead of going to the pubs. It's officially against the law to drink in public, but it's rarely enforced. In this case, though, it's a real Galway experience: this place is a real social hub of the city.

CHAPTER ONE

History of GALWAY

Galway during the Middle Ages

In 1124, when a fort was built there, Galway was first written about. However, the town was not built until the 1300s. In 1170 and 1171, the English attacked the eastern part of Ireland. In 1232, a baron called Richard de Burgh took over this area and built a town there. After 1270, Galway was surrounded by walls.

In 1396, Galway got a charter, which gave the people of the town certain rights. The city of Galway became a royal town. The city got a mayor in 1484. Around 3,000 people lived in Galway at that time. By today's standards, it looks like a small village, but back then, it was a medium-sized town.

The 14 families who ran Galway for hundreds of years were known as the tribes of Galway. From these 14 families generally came the mayor and the most important people in the town.

They were the families of Athy, Blake, Bodkin, Browne, Darcy, Deane, French, Font, Joyce, Kirwan, Lynch, Martin, Morris, and Skerrett.

Galway was an important port in the Middle Ages. The wine was the main source. They sent things like wool, skins, and leather overseas. But the most important people in Galway had English manners and habits. During the 14th and 15th centuries, the English kings lost control of most of Ireland, except for Dublin and the Pale area around it. But Galway was, in a lot of ways, an island of "Englishness."

In 1473 and 1500, there were two very bad fires in Galway. (Fire was always a risk because most houses were made of wood and had straw roofs. But if a building burned down, it would be easy to build a new one.

In 1320, they built the Church of St. Nicholas, and in 1296, Franciscan friars came to Galway. Friars were like monks, but instead of staying away from the world, they went out to teach. Because their clothes were grey, Franciscan friars were called "grey friars."

In 1488, the Dominicans, or "black friars" came next. In 1508, Augustinian friars came to the area.

Lynch window is a memorial to James Lynch Fitzstephen, who, legend has it, killed his son in 1493 and hung him from a tree.

Galway between 1500 and 1800

Galway was still a wealthy town and port in the 1600s. Wine was still the main product. Some of Galway's streets were paved in 1505.

Also, Galway got new charters in 1545, which made the Aran Island part of its territory. In 1579, Galway got another charter. A writer at the time said, "The town is well built and walled, has a good harbor and is full of wealthy merchants."

In 1543, St. Bridget's Hospital was built. That year, there was a lot of sweaty sickness in Galway. Nobody knows for sure what this disease was, but it killed a lot of people in the city. But Galway quickly got better and started to do well again.

The Spanish Arch was built in 1584, and Lynch's Castle is a house that was built around 1600. The only thing left of a merchant's house built in the early 1700s is the Browne Doorway.

James I gave Galway another charter in 1610, which made the city and the 2 miles of land around it a separate county.

But Galway had a lot of trouble in 1649 when the plague hit the city. There were a lot of deaths. Then, in August of 1651, the English, led by General Edmund Ludlow, put Galway under siege. In April 1652, after a long siege, the town finally gave up.

Galway stayed a wealthy city through the 17th and 18th centuries. At the end of the 18th century, suburbs began to grow outside the city walls.

Galway back in the 1800s

At the start of the 19th century, about 5,000 people were living in Galway. However, that number went down during the 19th century. During the potato famine of 1845–1849, the whole area was affected badly, and a lot of people died.

Still, there were some changes for the better in Galway. In 1812, the Galway Courthouse was built, and in 1818, the Salmon Weir Bridge was built. In 1849, Queens College Galway first opened. In 1850, the railroad reached Galway. But in the 19th century, a lot of the people who lived in Galway were poor and dirty.

GALWAY TODAY

Galway came back to life in the 20th century. By 1950, about 21,000 people were living there. Still, Galway was a busy port. Farm goods, wool, and marble were among the things that were sent abroad. In the 20th century, iron, milling, furniture making, and hat making were all done in Galway.

At the end of the 20th century, Galway's traditional businesses started to be replaced by more modern ones like engineering, IT, and electronics.

In 1934, a figure of Padraic O'Conaire was put up. Kennedy Park is named for President John F. Kennedy, who came to Galway in 1963.

In 1957, John J. Robinson made plans for the Roman Catholic Cathedral in Galway. It was done in the year 1965. In 1977, the Galway City Museum opened, and in 1984, the Quincentennial Fountain was built. Galway is now an important place to shop in the area. In 1991, Eyre Shopping Center opened.

In the past few years, Galway's economy has grown and its population has grown quickly. In 2022, 80,307 people in Galway.

Top 20 Things to Do in GALWAY, Sightseeing, Attractions, and Landmarks & Insider Tips

The Burren (Irish)

The Burren is a huge, surreal area of scarred and fissured limestone rock that is more than 115 square miles (300 square kilometers) in size and has been formed by acidic erosion. Even though it looks empty from far away, this rocky area is full of life. In the spring and summer, rare and wild plants grow well here.

Castle of Dunguaire

The 16th-century Dunguaire Castle is on a cliff that sticks out into Galway Bay. It looks like something out of a fairy story to people driving along the coast road, so many of them stop and pull out their cameras. Before famous Irish surgeon, poet, and writer Oliver St. John Gogarty bought it in 1924, it was home to important clans in the area for hundreds of years. He then made it a place where Ireland's best writers, like Lady Gregory, W.B. Yeats, Seán O'Casey, and George Bernard Shaw, liked to hang out. Most tourists look at the castle from afar today, but some do go inside.

Galway Bay

Galway Bay is on the west coast of Ireland. It is fed by the Atlantic Ocean and washes up on some of the country's most beautiful shorelines. At its edge are the three windswept Aran Islands. The bay meets the mainland at the artsy city of Galway and several fishing towns, cliffs, and beaches.

Kylemore Abbey and the Victorian Walled Garden

The neo-Gothic Kylemore Abbey and Victorian Walled Garden look just like a castle from a fairytale. It is right on the edge of Kylemore Lake. When the abbey was built in 1868, grateful locals who were still hurting from the Irish Potato Famine worked on it. The Benedictine nuns who live there now let people into parts of the house and the grounds.

The Connemara

Connemara, which stretches from Galway to the Atlantic Ocean, is Ireland at its most rocky and natural. It is wild, and beautiful, and has few people living there. The Atlantic coast is broken up by beaches and small towns, and the interior is made up of bog, mountains, lakes, and empty areas with more sheep than people.

The Spanish Arch

The Spanish Arch is a Galway feature on the banks of the River Corrib. It is all that is left of a bastion built to protect the city in the late 1600s. The Spanish Arch is right in the middle of Galway, close to other city sites like the Claddagh and the Galway City Museum.

Sky Road

Clifden's Sky Road, a seven-mile drive, offers stunning views of Connemara and the Atlantic Sea. The road leads to the town of Clifden and its famous spires, 12 Bens Hills, and the distant islands. Every turn leads to an old castle or historic house, including the Gothic-style Clifden Castle. Memorial Hill offers a great view of Clifden, and the road can reach 500 feet above sea level. The Sky Road is considered one of Ireland's most beautiful drives.

The Medieval Banquet at Dunguaire Castle

The Medieval Banquet at Dunguaire Castle is an evening of music, stories, and traditional food and drink. The 500-year-old castle was once the home of powerful lords in the Middle Ages. It is on the southeast shore of Galway Bay. Today, if you want to have a good time, go to the medieval-themed banquet hall of the beautiful castle.

The Town of Salthill

Salthill is a popular Irish seaside town on the edge of Galway Bay. It is known for its sandy beaches and windswept coast. There are bars, restaurants, and hotels along a two-kilometer seafront walkway that has great views in every direction. During the summer, both locals and tourists come to swim, lay out in the sun, go on boats, and fish.

Omey Island

Omey Island is a Galway secret that not many people know about. It's in Connemara, near Claddaghduff, and you can only get there when the tide is low. Check the tide times ahead of time!

You can walk, ride a bike, or drive to the island. It's a great place to go if you're looking for things to do in Galway that will get you away from the crowds and into a beautiful natural area.

Around Omey, you can go on several different walks, but make sure you know how the waves work before you go.

Killary Fjord

I've been wanting to try this for a long time! The Killary Fjord is a place that looks like it was taken right out of a picture. It's beautiful, untouched, and quiet when there aren't five buses parked in Leenaun.

Several companies offer boat tours of the harbor, and those who go on them can see amazing views of the area. Try one of the Killary boat tours if you're looking for something different to do in Galway.

Quiet Man Bridge

The Quiet Man Bridge is for people who have seen the John Wayne and Maureen O'Hara movie of the same name.

A lot of the movie was shot in Cong, which is in Mayo, but some parts were also shot in Connemara. The Quiet Man Bridge is on the N59 going west, about 8 km past Oughterard. Even if you haven't seen the show, you should stop by for a moment.

Trad Pubs In Galway City

Many lists of things to do in Galway will include things to do with drinks. And with good cause. Some of the best bars in the country are in Galway.

I think the cozy but very busy Tigh Neachtains is the best of Galway City's many (and I mean many) bars. Another great place is the Crane Bar, especial lly if you want to go to a folk music session.

Athenry Castle

Athenry Castle is one of the best castles to see in Galway, and it's a great place to start learning about the past of the city. It is where the town began, and from there it has grown. There have been a lot of arguments about when the castle was first built. Richard de Burgo, Lord of Connaught, gave Meiler be Bermingham, Second Baron of Athenry, a charter to build his castle sometime after 1235. Most records say it happened in 1238, but there is enough evidence to show it could also have happened in 1240.

The castle was in ruins for more than 500 years. In 1990, the National Monuments section of the Office of Public Works decided to start fixing it up. Today, it stands tall over the town and looks beautiful both during the day and at night, when the spotlights shine on this beautiful landmark. It still stands today, which is a tribute to the people who worked to fix it

Aran Islands

This group of three beautiful, lightly populated islands is a stronghold of traditional Irish culture. They are located off Ireland's rocky, windy Atlantic coast on the western edge of Europe. The Aran Islands' jagged coastal rocks surround a patchwork of green fields, where the remains of ancient stone forts and medieval churches can be seen. In their one- and two-pub towns, people talk about local news in Irish Gaelic (Gaeilge), and traditional music sessions go on late into the night.

Galway Cathedral

Galway Cathedral was built in the 1960s. It is one of the youngest stone churches in Ireland and one of the youngest in Europe. Even though it was built in the 20th century, the church has details from the Renaissance, Romanesque, and Gothic styles, as well as Irish artwork and decorations.

Poulnabrone Portal Tomb (Poulnabrone Dolmen)

The Poulnabrone Dolmen, a long slab of rock put horizontally on top of several upright slabs, has stood on this lonely limestone plateau for 5,000 years. It is one of Ireland's most photographed ancient sites. It marks the spot of a group grave where the bodies of people who lived between 3800 BC and 3200 BC were buried.

Galway City Museum

This museum is all about Galway's past. It has displays on everything from the traditional Galway hooker boat to famous writers from the area. Some of the things in the collection are stone ax heads from the Stone Age, a cannonball from the Middle Ages, and the death warrant for a local man named Myles Joyce, who was wrongly hanged for murder in 1882.

Lough Corrib

Lough Corrib is a 69-square-mile lake in the west of Ireland. It is in both County Galway and County Mayo. People go there to fish, especially for brown trout and salmon that live in the wild. Over the ages, the lake has been a source of inspiration for many writers and artists. Oscar Wilde's father, the historian William Wilde, even wrote a book about Lough Corrib.

The Town of Clonmacnoise

This monastery was started by St. Ciarán in the sixth century and is in a green field next to the River Shannon. It was a center for Christian learning in Ireland. The scattered stone ruins, which include a cathedral, churches, round towers, high crosses, and grave markers, still have a spiritual feel.

CHAPTER TWO

GALWAY Essentials

(Languages, Plug Types, Electricity, Currency, International dialing codes, Emergency Telephone number, Visa Requirement)

Ireland has both English and Irish as its main languages. But the majority of people in Galway know English. Even though many people still speak Irish and it is taught in schools, most people in Galway talk to each other every day in English. Locals know English, so tourists won't have any trouble getting around and using the city's services and attractions.

Types of Plugs and Electricity: Ireland uses type G plugs, which have three square prongs. The power is 50 hertz (Hz) and 230 volts (AC). You'll need a plug adapter if you're going from somewhere other than Europe. It's important to know that plug adapters are easy to find at most travel or tech stores. It's also a good idea. to make sure that your electronics can work with the 230-volt AC power source to avoid any damage.

Ireland uses the euro (€) as its currency. Banks, exchange offices, and even some places let you change money. Most places will let you pay with a credit card or debit card. It's best to let your bank or credit card company know you're going to be traveling so you can use your cards without any problems. Also, you should always bring some cash with you in case you come across places that only take cash.

International calling code: The international calling code for Ireland is +353. When calling Ireland from outside the country, make sure to put +353 before the local phone number. Also, it's important to know that some mobile phone companies charge roaming fees for calls made from abroad, so it's best to check with your service ahead of time or think about getting a local SIM card for cheaper ways to talk.

Number to Call in an Emergency: In Ireland, the number to call in an emergency is 112. You can call this number for any kind of emergency, such as a medical emergency, an accident, or a crime. It's important to keep this number close by in case something goes wrong.

Visas: Most people can stay in Ireland for up to 90 days without a visa. But before you go on a trip, you should always check with your office or port. It's also a good idea to have travel insurance that covers medical bills and situations while you're in Ireland. Also, it's a good idea to have a hard copy or digital copy of your passport and other important papers in case you lose or have them stolen while you're away.

Prices in GALWAY (lunch and drinks, Transportation, Accommodation, best hotels)

Lunch and drinks:

Lunch: €10-15 per person

Drinks: €4-6 per drink

Transportation:

Bus: €1.50-2.50 per ride

Taxi: €10-15 for a short ride within the city

Accommodation:

Hostel: €20-30 per night

Budget hotel: €50-75 per night

Mid-range hotel: €100-150 per night

Luxury hotel: €200+ per night

Festivals in GALWAY

Galway City is the cultural heart of Ireland. It has fairs and events that are known all over the world all year long. You can find all of these things and more in Galway, whether you're looking for art that will change you, things that will amaze kids, or a day at the races.

Here is a list of 11 fairs and events in Galway that will make your trip to the city more fun.

Galway Christmas Market in November and December

At the Galway Christmas Market, you can wear your most gaudy Geansa Nollaig and enjoy all things holiday. From November, Eyre Square is filled with huts full of gift ideas and garlands that twinkle. International foods like sausages and crêpes can take the edge off your shopping hunger.

Walk through the magical light gardens and stop to listen to live music. In the middle of the market, there is a 32-meter-high Big Wheel, a classic carousel, and Santa's Express Train. These are all fun for people of all ages.

Christmas Market in Galway: The Galway Christmas Market is one of the largest and most popular Christmas markets in Ireland. It is held in Eyre Square from late November to early December, and it features over 100 stalls selling everything from Christmas gifts to food and drink.

Cirt International Literature Festival

April

The Cirt International Festival of Literature gives readers and artists a place to talk, think, and argue. At the Galway Arts Centre and the Town Hall Theatre, you can meet a new author or see an old favorite. The focus of this event, which is one of the oldest in Europe, is on both Irish and international writing.

Past highlights include a revealing conversation with Marian Keyes, Emma Dabiri talking about What White People Can Do Next with Blindboy Boatclub, and Mind Your Language: Having a Word with Ourselves, which looked at the connections between Ireland's two languages.

Cirt International Literature Festival: The Cirt International Literature Festival is a week-long festival that celebrates the written word. It is held in April, and it features a variety of events, including readings, workshops, and panel discussions with authors from all over the world.

Festival of Early Music in Galway

May

Since 1996, the Galway Early Music Festival has been going on in May to show off the best music from the Middle Ages, the Renaissance, and the Baroque. Through performances by Irish and foreign artists, the city's streets and venues are filled with songs that have been around for hundreds of years.

You could try playing a traditional Irish harp or take a singing walk around Galway in the 17th century with the Spanish Captain Moreno. Concerts, displays, and talks at places like St. Nicholas' Collegiate Church of Ireland take you on a world tour of early sounds.

Festival of early music in Galway: The Galway Early Music Festival is a two-week festival that showcases the best of early music from the Middle Ages, Renaissance, and Baroque periods. It is held in May, and it features concerts, workshops, and lectures at a variety of venues throughout the city.

Trad at the Prom

From May to September

Go to Salthill to be swept away by this show of music, song, and dance. At Trad on the Prom in the Leisureland Theatre, world-champion Irish dancers, talented multi-instrumentalists, and award-winning singers give it their all. From May to September, you can see great Irish entertainment that follows in the proud footsteps of shows like Riverdance. Before you know it, you'll be tapping your toes.

Trad at the Prom: Trad at the Prom is a free outdoor concert series that takes place every summer in Salthill. It features a variety of traditional Irish musicians, and it is a great way to experience Irish culture.

The Galway Sessions

June

Celebrate the Irish songs we've shared with the rest of the world. In June, folk tales bring pipes, fiddles, and concertinas to life. The Sessions is an annual summer event that brings people from all over the world to Galway. Some of the performers come from Stirling, Scotland, which shows that the two cities share a cultural bond.

There are events at the Town Hall Theatre and in bars like The Crane Bar, The Quays Bar, and The Kings Head all over the city.

The Galway Sessions: The Galway Sessions is a week-long festival that celebrates traditional Irish music. It is held in June, and it features concerts, workshops, and pub sessions all over the city.

Galway Film Fleadh

July

Every July, the Galway Film Fleadh is a treat for movie fans because it brings together audiences and artists. The Fleadh is a place for the most daring new movies to be shown, and entries come from all over the world. You can watch movies that are only being shown here and talk to stars like Brendan Gleeson and Anjelica Huston.

Galway Film Fleadh: The Galway Film Fleadh is an international film festival that focuses on new and independent films. It is held in July, and it features screenings, workshops, and discussions with filmmakers from all over the world.

International Arts Festival in Galway

July

The Galway International Arts Festival in July is an amazing arts event that includes all kinds of artistic expression. Events range from immersive displays to dance and theater groups from around the world. There are talks about the problems we face in a world that is changing, and top bands like The Academic, Sinéad O'Connor, and the Pixies play to excited crowds. One of the best places to dance and meet people is on the NUI Galway grounds, under the Heineken Big Top.

International Arts Festival in Galway: The Galway International Arts Festival is one of the largest and most prestigious arts festivals in Ireland. It is held in July, and it features a variety of events, including theater, dance, music, and visual arts.

Races in Galway

July

Galway Racecourse hosts the world-famous Galway Races Summer Festival every July. This event is always a hit with horse racing fans and people who just like to bet on horses. Race Days are the most exciting sporting event in Galway, and they also bring a lot of color and energy to the city. With Ladies Day and Weekender's elaborate fashion shows, there's something for everyone to get dressed up for.

Races in Galway: The Galway Races Summer Festival is a week-long horse racing festival that is held in July. It is one of the most popular sporting events in Ireland, and it attracts thousands of visitors from all over the world.

Galway's Oyster Festival is held every year.

September

The Galway International Oyster Festival is the granddaddy of seafood festivals. It is the oldest oyster festival in the world and one of the oldest food festivals in Europe. Gather in September for the World Oyster Opening Championships to watch world-class entertainment and cheer for your favorite. On the Galway Oyster Festival Seafood Trail, people who like all kinds of seafood can also eat their way around the city.

Galway International Oyster Festival: The Galway International Oyster Festival is a seafood festival that is held in September. It is one of the oldest and largest oyster festivals in the world, and it features oyster tastings, cooking demonstrations, and live music.

Baboró International Children's Arts Festival

October

In October, the Baboró International Arts Festival for Children takes over theaters, galleries, and public areas in Galway. Plays, workshops, storytelling, and much more offer something for people of all kinds.

Stories are told through a mix of comedy and music, and you can get involved through dance and visual art that is bright, engaging, and lively. A wide range of programs in places like the Mick Lally Theatre will open people's minds and hearts.

Baboró International Children's Arts Festival: The Baboró International Children's Arts Festival is a week-long festival that celebrates children's creativity. It is held in October, and it features a variety of events, including theater, dance, music, and visual arts.

Galway Festival of Comedy

October

In October, the Galway Comedy Festival brings both well-known and up-and-coming actors to the stage. Ireland's biggest comedy event has more than 80 acts over a week. International and Irish comedians like Reginald D. Hunter and Ardal O'Hanlon are among the guests. Book a table at Faulty Towers:

The Dining Experience for dinner with a smile. Basil, Sybil, and Manuel serve up a meal from the 1970s and lots of improvised jokes in a very messy way.

Galway Festival of Comedy: The Galway Festival of Comedy is a week-long comedy festival that features a variety of Irish and international comedians. It is held in October, and it is one of the most popular comedy festivals in Ireland.

Galway, which is on the west coast of Ireland, is known
for its many events. During the Middle Ages, it was run
by 14 trading families. So, Galway became a very
important port. It was chosen as the European Capital of
Culture for 2020 and shines all over Europe.

Galway is the most Irish city in the Republic of Ireland,
if there is such a thing. Galway is often called the cultural
heart of Ireland because it is in an area where most people
speak Gaelic as their first language and have a strong love
for culture, music, and dance. Galway is on the Atlantic
water, so the water is as much a part of the city's culture
as the culture itself, and the city's many students give it a
lively, bohemian feel. So, let's go see what Galway has to
offer.

City of Tribes

City of Tribes is the name of the city. These tribes were
14 merchant families that ran the city's politics, business,
and social life. The Athy, Blake, Bodkin, Browne,
D'Arcy, Deane, Font, Ffrench, Joyce, Kirwan, Lynch,
Martin, Morris, and Skerritt all had a lot of power,
especially during the Middle Ages and the Early Modern
Period. During the English takeover of Ireland, the name

"The Tribes of Galway" was made up as a way to insult the people, but the families took it as a sign of defiance and used it.

If you walk along Eyre Square, you will see the flags of the families flying high. If you come across a navy blue roundabout, look for the writing on it. It is also named after one of the families.

The Wall in the Mall

Galway used to have a wall, just like many towns in Europe did in the Middle Ages. Even though that wall has been taken down for a long time, you can still see some pieces of it. One of the best-preserved pieces is... inside a shopping mall! And it's quite a sight to see since a piece of the wall and a couple of towers are part of the Eyre Square Centre and are covered by a high glass roof. What a strange thing!

Kicking the Wall

When it comes to walls, you can't leave Galway without kicking the Salthill Promenade wall. Locals call it "The Prom," and it's a 2-kilometer walk along the coast. It's a great way to relax, get some sea air, and watch the sunset from the sand or one of the many bars or restaurants. Just don't forget to kick the wall in front of the Blackrock Diving Tower before you turn around. It's supposed to bring luck, so any real Galwegian wouldn't miss it. Also, six years ago, a gift box was put in place so that people could give money to Galway's charities.

Where is that bar from "Galway Girl"?

If you're like us, you couldn't help but think of Ed Sheeran's song "Galway Girl," which is about an English guy who visits the city and falls in love with a local who plays the fiddle. Saoirse Ronan plays the "Galway Girl" in the video, which is shot from her point of view. It shows us a night out in the town, especially in a pub, which is the real star of the video, if you ask us. Where is it, though? Well, it turns out that it is in Salthill, and the pub is called "O'Connor's." The same family has run it since 1942! Inside, there are different rooms, one of which looks like a ship and the other like a house. Every night, music is played. In the end, it is Ireland.

St Nicholas' Collegiate Church

Since it is in the middle of town, there is a good chance that you will visit the ancient St. Nicholas' Collegiate Church while you are in Galway. The past of this Anglican Episcopalian church is pretty interesting. It began as a Catholic church for Nicholas of Myrna, the patron saint of sailors. People say that Christopher Columbus went to church in Galway when he stopped there on his journey.

In 1652, Cromwell's English men ended the siege of Galway, and the church was turned into a stable. The English men will damage the statues on the building, except for one smiling angel. It is now a church for everyone. Its minister is a woman named Lynda Pellow, and it was the first church in Ireland to bless a same-sex couple in public. Also, people know that the church puts on a lot of singing events. The church has its choir school, and it also holds shows often.

Trains make it easy to get to Galway:

Galway is easy to get to by train. Central Square is right next to the main bus stops and train station. If you fly into Dublin, you might want to take the train to Galway instead of getting a car there. It can help you save some money. The church is known for more than just its lively music scene. It is also known for its openness and progressive ideals. It actively supports diversity and equality, which makes it a place where everyone can feel welcome. Whether you want to go to a service or enjoy a musical show, this church gives visitors and locals alike a unique and welcoming experience.

Plan for at Least Two Days

To see everything in Galway, you'll need at least two full days. Even though it's a small, easy-to-get-to city, there's a lot to see and do there. Also, Galway is a good starting point for day trips to places like the Aran Islands and the Cliffs of Moher, which are both fun places to visit. Galway has a lively arts and culture scene with many galleries, theaters, and events to enjoy. Don't miss the Galway International Arts Festival, which has many different shows and acts. The city is also known for its lively nightlife. There are a lot of pubs and places with live music to go to at nighnight

Always a small city that is easy to get around on foot.

You won't need a car to enjoy its charms, except for places like the BlackRock diving board that are outside of the city center but can still be reached by bike. It's easy to walk around Galway's shops, restaurants, and historic places because the streets are made for people. Also, the city's infrastructure makes it easy for people to ride bikes through its beautiful neighborhoods and enjoy the beautiful scenery in the nearby areas.

Galway has a lot of great places to eat that are both tasty and cheap.

Do your homework and make reservations ahead of time, especially at famous restaurants. Locals go to these places often. Try getting there early if you can't get a ticket. Galway is a small city, so it's easy to walk to places and ask if they have space. Galway is known not only for its great restaurants but also for its lively food markets and street food scene. People can look around the busy shops at the Galway Market or grab a quick bite to eat at one of the city's many food trucks. Galway has something for every taste and price, whether you want traditional Irish food or food from around the world.

Galway is a lively city with a lot of great energy, and there is a lot of live music to go along with it.

Traditional Irish music is played in many pubs, and you can find live cover bands and buskers in many places. It's a great place for people who like to listen to music, and it's easier to find live music here than in Dublin. Galway has a lot of different kinds of music, like rock, jazz, and folk, as well as native Irish music. Throughout the year, the city has many music festivals that draw both local and foreign musicians. Galway is a great place to see live music, whether you're looking for a cozy pub or a larger venue for a show.

Boat to the Aran Islands

You can take a boat from Galway to the Aran Islands for a day trip or to stay there for the night. From the city, it's easy to get there. People know the Aran Islands for their beautiful landscapes and deep cultural history. People can visit old sites, hike along beautiful cliffs, and learn about traditional Irish culture. Taking a boat to the Aran Islands is something that everyone who goes to Galway must do.

Day Trip to Cliffs of Moher

You can go to the Cliffs of Moher from Galway on a day trip. It takes about two and a half hours by city bus, but there are many day trips from Galway if you'd rather not deal with the trouble.

Best Seasons to Visit GALWAY

When to go to Galway City

Plan your trip to Ireland carefully by thinking about the weather and events that will be going on during the time you want to go.

The Weather in Ireland

Even though Ireland is about as far north as Newfoundland, it has a mild, wet climate because of the southwest winds that blow there most of the time and the warm Gulf Stream that flows along its western coast. Since no part of the island is more than 110 km (70 miles) from the sea, temperatures are pretty even all over the country.

- January is the worst month for weather. On average, it is 6°C in the morning and 144mm of rain falls in January.
- The weather is bad from February to April. Every month, it rains about 84mm and is about 12°C at lunchtime.

- From May to October, the weather is okay, but not great. The highest temperature is 14°C°C, and each month it rains about 122mm.

- November is a bad month for the weather. By early evening, the average temperature is 8°C, and it rains an average of 149mm per month during this time.

- In December, the weather is the worst it can be. In December, it gets as warm as 9°C°C and rains about 37% of the time.

Because of the Atlantic winds, parts of the west of the country get twice as much rain as the east. The average amount of rain that falls each year is 1,500mm (59 inches).

From November to February, you should stay away from rural Ireland. It can be cold and wet everywhere, and the days are short, lasting from about 8:30 a.m. to 4:3 p.m But city breaks at that time of year can be very nice, especially since many bars and restaurants have open fires that add to the atmosphere.

Ireland has both busy and slow times.

Most Irish families go on vacation in July and August, which is also when most British families go on vacation. Prices go up, and so does the pressure on infrastructure. Late spring and early fall are the best times to go.

Outside of the busy season, you can get great deals on bed and breakfasts, especially if you stay for two or more nights. In the summer, places along the coast will be busy, but from October or November to mid-March or April, many smaller guesthouses and restaurants close in more rural places like the Ring of Kerry and Connemara.

Galway's busiest times and times with the most tourists

Find out when Galway's high tourist season when the most people visit and low tourist season is by looking at the facts and numbers provided below.

Galway has tourist times.

Galway has a very slow season.

January, February, and March are the months with the fewest people.

Galway's off-season

April and November are the months with the fewest people.

Galway's busy season

In May, June, September, October, and December, a lot of people come to Galway.

Galway's busiest time is

July and August are the months when most people come to Galway.

CHAPTER THREE

GALWAY Packing List: Essential Things to Pack for Galway (And What to Wear)

Are you wondering what to wear in Ireland and what clothing in Ireland is best? This section of this guide is here to help you in making your decision on what to wear. While Ireland is known for its lush green landscapes and inclement weather, it doesn't have to impact your wardrobe choices.

With all that weather, there are some beautiful things to see. It's hard not to love the country with its green rolling hills, crumbling castles, dramatic coastlines, friendly people, and lovely farms.

Don't let bad weather stop you. Ireland doesn't have bad weather; people just wear the wrong clothes. We talk about our favorite things to bring to Ireland for a comfortable and smart trip. This guide should have something for everyone, whether it's your first time traveling or you've been all over the world.

Tips For Packing For Galway, Ireland

There are a few essentials that I think everyone should bring on their trip. Ireland is known for being wet, so what you pack in your bag or suitcase will depend a lot on the weather. Don't worry, though. Most Irish people are down-to-earth, so simple clothes will make you feel right at home. There are always a few exceptions, like a night at the Abbey Theatre in Dublin or a great meal in Galway.

We wear a sweater, pants, boots, and a rain jacket most of the time in Ireland. We, like most travelers, will spend most of our time outside experiencing the countryside of Ireland. It has old walking paths, castles, cozy pubs, sheep, and quaint towns. It's the perfect place to get lost.

- Always bring a rain jacket, an umbrella, and boots that can handle the weather.
- Packing cubes help keep wet or dirty clothes from getting mixed up with clean ones.
- You should bring no more than three pairs of shoes: a nice pair, a casual pair, and a pair of sports shoes or boots.
- Ireland is a laid-back place, so unless you're staying at one of the famous sports resorts, there's no need to dress up.
- It's sweater weather almost all the time, so bring your best wool sweater or cardigan.

- If it's cold outside, a scarf and hat are great ways to stay warm.

Not all the time is it cold. The weather in the summer can be warm and beautiful. Check the weather forecast ahead of time and bring clothes for warm weather. We've had great weather on trips and bad weather that made us wonder if we should even go to Ireland.

Ireland's weather

Find out what the weather will be like in Ireland before you decide what to pack. Ireland has an oceanic climate, which means that it is always cool, damp, and wet. During the year, there aren't many big changes in the weather. A hot day in the summer is just as rare as snow in the winter. This is good news for packing since you won't have to bring clothes for different weather conditions.

Checking the weather in Ireland a week before your trip will give you the best idea of what the temperatures will be like.

Seasons in Ireland

Spring	Springtime in Ireland is a very chilly time of year. March to April is frigid, and things start to warm up by May. We love spring as it is the driest time of year.
Summer	From June to August, temperatures mix warm and cool with frequent rain showers. The average daily highs are around 19/20C (66/68F), with cool evenings. There is the occasional sunny day with temperatures mid-25C or 77F, if not warmer.
Fall	September to November can be the rainiest and windiest time of year. Temperatures continue to fall from the more mild summer. Expect 10-17C (50-63F) for daytime highs in the fall.
Winter	The weather can be cold during the winter, but it rarely reaches below freezing. It's often cloudy, and the winds can be powerful. At night temperatures are a few degrees above freezing, and the daytime sees temperatures around 7-10C (45-50F).

Essential Documents To Pack

Passport: It's clear, but without a passport, you won't get very far.

Credit Cards: When we travel, we always use several credit cards that cover our purchases, give us rewards, and don't charge us any fees when we use them abroad.

Visa: If you need a visa, make sure you have one.

Debit Cards: In Ireland, it's a good idea to carry euros. We never change our money at places with bad exchange rates. Instead, when we get there, we use the ATM.

There are low or no overseas transaction fees at Charles Schwab, Ally, and Capital One. Keep in mind that the Euro is used in the Republic of Ireland and the Great British Pound is used in Northern Ireland.

Driving License: If you want to rent a car, you'll need your driver's license, and it never hurts to have a second form of I.D. If your license is not in English, you may need an IDP translation into English.

What Should You Pack for Ireland?

We can suggest two bags for a trip to Europe. You can choose between a standard hard-shell suitcase with four wheels or a travel backpack.

The best suitcases have four wheels, so they can be rolled sideways down the aisle of a train or a path. We like hard shells because they protect and keep us safe better. The Delsey Helium Aero 25″ is our best hard-shell bag.

Travel backpacks are great for young tourists, digital nomads, and minimalists. They are also great if you want to save money on any fees your airline might charge you for checked bags.

How Should I Dress in Ireland?

Wool Pullover

The wool sweater is the one piece of clothing made in Ireland that is good for traveling. A sweater is a great piece to have in your trip wardrobe. They look good, feel good, and keep you warm. It doesn't matter what time of year it is because most of Ireland is always cool and pleasant. During the summer, the days will be warm, but the nights will be cool.

I have a lot of sweaters, but the ones I like best are made of natural materials like wool or alpaca. It's my favorite thing to bring back from a trip, and I love my Scottish wool and Peruvian alpaca sweaters.

Ireland has some great wool and jumper makers, but you might have to look a little bit to find them. In recent years, many tourist shops have sold cheap copies made in other countries.

A raincoat

As soon as you're done packing your wool sweater, grab a rain jacket. If we were betting, we'd bet that it will rain on you while you're in Ireland. It needs a lot of rain to get that green. Ireland has a wide range of rain. Some days, it might only rain in the afternoon, while other times, a storm might last for days.

We recommend a raincoat that can be folded up and is made for the woods and hiking. They are light, long-lasting, easy to pack, windproof, and waterproof. Any raincoat will do, but the expensive ones made for the outdoors will last longer and be more useful in bad weather. They are also very good at stopping the wind, which can be very strong.

Flannel Shirts

Men and women both look great in flannel shirts worn in middle layers. Nice cotton keeps you warm, makes you feel good, and looks good. They are very easy to dress up or down for a casual outdoor look. A cozy flannel is great for sightseeing, traveling, or going on short walks.

Most of Ireland is very laid-back, so a flannel or sweater will make you feel right at home. You can look classic and stay warm by wearing a shirt with a travel vest. It's simple to put in any bag.

A down coat

In the summer, visitors might be able to stay warm with just a wool sweater and a rain jacket. A down jacket is a great idea for any season other than summer. On a trip with cool weather, we suggest bringing a down jacket that you can pack up.

A down jacket is a great way to stay warm in a place like Ireland without taking up too much room in your suitcase. If you want a more fashionable jacket, a peacoat is a classic choice, but it's bulky, so you'll have to wear it on the plane.

A T-Shirt

A basic T-shirt will always be in style. We recommend using solid shades like black, white, and grey. When we go hiking on a sunny day, it can get pretty hot, so we often take off some clothes. If you already have a few technical shirts and want to go on casual hikes or walks around the town, a simple cotton t-shirt will do.

A merino wool shirt, on the other hand, is a good purchase and one of the best travel clothes. Wool shirts stay fresh longer and do a great job of keeping you at the right temperature.

Blue jeans

There are a lot of Irish people who wear jeans that fit well but are nothing big or torn. Jeans are a fashion staple, but they aren't the best pants for travel because they don't pack well or feel good. DU/ER jeans, on the other hand, are a good choice for tourists. The jeans made of organic cotton look nice, but a small amount of polyester and spandex makes them stretchy and keeps them from getting wrinkled.

The fit is great, and the leg is slim down. You can wear the jeans on long trip days without having to worry about being uncomfortable. The synthetic mix makes them great for long trips because you don't have to wash them.

Pants for Tech

If you want to move around Ireland, chinos or travel pants are great to have. Our first choice is a solid pair of "travel pants" made of synthetic materials. Most of the time, these pants don't get dirty easily, dry quickly, weigh less, stay clean for more than one wear, and are more comfortable than regular pants or chinos.

We love that these pants, which used to only be made for camping, now look like chinos. It's a basic pant that looks good with a sweater, dress shirt, t-shirt, or blouse. Try to pick a color that goes with the place you're going and the time of year. But pants that are light tan tend to be the most useful.

For women, we recommend the Kuhl Freeflex Pants for outdoor activities and the Everlane Utility Barrel Pants for a more stylish look in the city or town. Men should check out the KUHL Renegade Rock Pants for outdoor activities and the Western Rise Evolution 2.0 Pants for everything else.

A scarf

A scarf is a must-have for travel and a great choice of clothing for both men and women going to Ireland. They go with your outfit and keep you warm. They are also very comfy. The scarf covers your neck from the wind, which is common in Ireland.

Scarves are great for tourists because they can spice up an outfit you've worn three days in a row and can be thrown into a bag or purse to pull out when the sun goes down and it gets cold.

Sneakers

One of the best ways to get to know a new place is to walk around on the path and watch the city or town unfold around you. When packing for Ireland, both men and women need to make sure they have a pair of shoes that are comfortable.

I wouldn't suggest bringing those awful, bulky hiking shoes or sports shoes that a lot of tourists like to bring. Since most towns and cities in Ireland are nice places to walk around, you should bring good walking shoes. Allbirds Wool Runners are our best travel shoes because they are eco-friendly, warm, simple, and comfortable.

Shoes or Boots

Bring a lightweight pair of hiking boots or leather boots to help you deal with the rain. People in the area like to wear big rubber boots called "Wellies" or "Wellington Boots." We don't go to farms or bogs, so we can always be happy with good boots.

I love basic boots and can't get enough of leather boots. If you want the best boots for Ireland at a good price, check out Clark's or Timberland for leather boots. Check out Chippewa, Danner, or Red Wing boots made in the United States if you want good boots that will last a lifetime.

Underwear for travel

It would be best to bring several pairs of sports or travel underwear. We usually bring between five and seven pairs of underwear on a trip. We suggest that you get several pairs of wool or synthetic underwear.

Because these materials are antifungal, they stay fresh longer and dry fast if you wash them by hand. For women, it's best not to wear cheap cotton undies like most people do. Hygiene is very important for women, so antibacterial underwear is a lifesaver when you're out and about in the heat.

Socks

With a good pair of socks, we've learned to love our feet. When you walk around, you will want to keep your feet dry. The best thing about wool socks is that they stay fresh for several days because they are naturally resistant to bacteria. On every trip, we bring several sets of wool socks.

A pair of sunglasses

Sunglasses that look good are a great way to finish off an outfit. At least one pair of sunglasses belongs to everyone. But for the health of your eyes, it's best to make sure they protect against UV light.

We always bring two pairs of sunglasses when we go somewhere because we're pretty busy. A pair of Smith Optics for climbing and other outdoor activities and a stylish pair of sunglasses for the beach or a day out in town.

What Women Should Bring to Ireland

A coat.

I think you should get a peacoat if you want to look smart and stay warm. A peacoat is a great way to stay warm and look stylish. Even though we love our down jackets because they keep us warm and are easy to carry, they aren't the most stylish things in the world, and you'd look funny wearing one with a dress or suit.

Long-Sleeved Sweater

One of my favorite things to wear in Ireland is a sweater. A sweater looks and feels great, and it keeps you warm.

They are also small enough that they don't take up much space in the bag. It always good to bring one to Ireland because you can wear it with a coat in the winter and it rarely gets too hot in the summer.

Button-down shirt

Even though Ireland is a casual place, people still look nice when they go out. On cold days, most women wear a nice dress shirt, blouse, or jacket. On a rare warm summer day, they'll put on a summer dress.

Most women should avoid wearing graphic tees or short-sleeved shirts and instead wear a light top. The right blouse is very cool and comfy, so it's a great thing to wear in the summer.

Merino wool that isn't tied together

A Merino wool shirt is a good piece of trip clothing to buy. Even though it's more expensive, I've switched a lot of my clothes to it. Wool shirts stay fresh longer and do a great job of keeping you at a comfortable temperature anywhere in Ireland.

It better than cotton shirts, which get greasy and heavy after one or two wears, but wool shirts last for days.

Pants with a fleece lining

Ireland can get very cold, especially from the end of October to about April. This is when I often wear fleece-lined leggings, which look great while walking around towns like Dublin or Galway and keep me extra warm. You can wear fleece-lined leggings just like regula r leggings and pair them with any sweater or jacket you own.

These are great because they keep you warm and don't wear out easily. They also have secret reflectors in the hem turn-ups to help you stay seen. On the outside, these are tightly knit so they look nice, but on the inside, they are stuffed with fleece. There are different types of Crash tights, but the solid black ones are my favorite because they go with everything.

Jumpsuit or romper

One of my favorite travel clothes is probably a romper because it's stylish, comfy, and useful. You can't go wrong with this, and I'd recommend packing at least one or two rompers for Ireland. They're great for a night out in Dublin and, surprisingly, look great with Irish clothes.

Flats in black

Having a pair of black flats in a bag is always a good idea. They look good, are comfortable, and take up little space in your suitcase. Stay away from heels, because many places have cobblestone streets, and you don't want to break your ankle trying to look good. Just let the locals show you how well they can walk in high heels.

What Men Should Bring to Ireland

A coat.

A smart peacoat will keep you warm, just like it does for women. Even though we love our down jackets because they keep us warm and are easy to carry, they aren't the most stylish things in the world, and you'd look funny wearing one with a dress or suit.

Dress shirt and jeans

You would look pretty silly going to a nice meal in Dublin in a T-shirt or a sweatshirt. Bring at least one nice outfit that fits your style with you when you travel. Your plans for going to Ireland will also have a big effect. Bluffworks makes dress clothes for guys that don't wrinkle and can't be stained. Also, they make great gifts.

Henley was a poet.

Ireland is a great place to wear a henley. It's light but keeps you warm from the wind, and it's a better choice than a long-sleeved print shirt or technical clothing.

Parts and pieces, *Pack for the day*

When going, you'll need a place to put your camera gear, hand sanitizers, papers, phones, and anything else you might need for a full day out. Over the years, we have tried out a huge number of daypacks and bags.

Bathroom Bag

It's always a good idea to keep your toiletries tidy and separate from your clothes. A grooming bag almost seems like a must-have for any trip. Also, Ireland has a lot of bathrooms that are small or crowded.

If you don't have much room on your table, a hanging toiletry bag is a great choice. This style of bag tends to be better organized than the standard one, with more places to put things.

Adapter for Travel

For the items on your list to bring to Ireland, you will need an adapter. We always keep one in our carry-on bags, so we can charge our devices when we get there or at the airport. For the United Kingdom, you'll need the British "Type G" three-prong adapter. Type C, F, and E adaptors are used in most of Europe.

If you want to take great pictures while you're on vacation in Ireland, you have to bring a good camera. We bring a lot of cameras with us. Still, the RX 100 is the one we all agree is the best.

There are different versions with different prices, but all of them are easy to use and anyone can use them. It also takes great pictures with a resolution of 20 megapixels and full manual settings.

Towel for Travel

We always bring a travel towel with us when we go somewhere. It's one of the most important things to buy if you're going abroad. They are small, antibacterial, and light, so you won't always need a new towel or have to wash yours all the time.

Backpackers need to bring their towels because most hotels don't have them. But they're also great for people who aren't on a tight budget and want to go on trips and tours.

Paperwhite Kindle

For people who love to read and travel, a Kindle is a must-have item. Even though we love real books, they are too big and heavy to fit in my bag. We just got the Kindle Paperwhite, and we love it.

It's small, can be used with a touch screen, and has a backlight so you can read at night without a sharp glare. It's hard to find a better way to warm up than by sitting next to a wood stove with a cup of tea and a good book.

GALWAY: A Guide to Ireland

We already spend a lot of time with our phones in our daily lives and when we're making plans for trips. When we get to a place like Ireland, we put the phone down and pick up a map to help us get around.

Cubes for packing

Packing cubes is the best way to keep your bag or suitcase in order. They are one of the most important things to pack because they help you keep your clothes and toiletries in order. Cubes also keep clothes from getting wrinkled and keep them folded.

Holder of a Passport

I recommend that women traveling alone bring a black purse that is stylish and safe from theft. Cameron keeps his passport and credit cards in a good passport case, so he never loses them.

WHAT SHOULD YOU NOT WEAR IN IRELAND?

Fanny Bag

We've talked about what to wear in Ireland, so now let's talk about what NOT to wear. First, and most commonly, a hip pack. When you wear a fanny pack, people will know you are a stranger.

Small clothes

Even though Ireland is quickly becoming one of the most modern countries in the world, it still has strong Catholic roots. There is still a lot of Irish Catholicism in the country, and people outside of the big cities tend to dress conservatively.

Wear for sports

We've already talked about this, but sports clothes are meant to be worn to the gym or when you're being active. If you're not going or coming from the gym, wearing sports Not long, tank tops, or running shoes will make you stand out. Don't get me wrong, you can wear whatever you want when it's hot outside, but it's easy for a stranger to pick on you because of it.

Shorts

Shorts aren't usually needed, so most Irish people don't wear them. Still, views are changing, and I'm sure that with global warming, they'll warm up to the idea.

White socks for sports

Most Europeans don't wear white socks that are too tall and show. Try to wear black socks with patterns or socks that match your pants.

Summary of What to Wear in Ireland

When going, it's best not to forget things like medicines, toiletries, and other things you might need. But there are plenty of shops in every Irish city and town. But this is a general list of what to bring to Ireland for everyone.

Don't forget that Ireland isn't the end of the world. If you forget something, you'll probably be able to find it there.

GALWAY Travel Requirements 2024

When we go on trips, it's important to know about the latest rules and regulations. A new travel rule called the ETIAS Visa (European Travel Information and Authorization System Visa) will go into effect in January 2024. This rule applies to people from the United States, the United Kingdom, Australia, Canada, and a few other English-speaking countries that are not in the EU. In this full guide, we'll go over everything you need to know about ETIAS to make sure your trips go smoothly and without stress.

What is ETIAS?

ETIAS is the European Travel Information and Authorization System Visa. It was made to make traveling in the European Union and the Schengen Zone safer and easier. Even though it sounds like a visa, ETIAS is a travel authorization or pass. It doesn't replace your passport or any other cards you may already have. Think of it as an extra layer of paperwork that will help make border control easier and make people safer.

Duration and Passport Validity

You can use an ETIAS Visa for three years after you get it. But it's important to know that its legality depends on when your passport expires.

If your passport ends before those three years are up, you'll need to renew both your passport and your ETIAS Visa at the same time. Make sure that your passport is still good at least three months after the date you plan to return.

Exemptions and Special Cases

EU members and people with proof of residency in any EU country don't need an ETIAS Visa. Always check the official ETIAS website for the most recent permits, as rules can change over time.

Visa Limitations

It's important to know that the ETIAS Visa doesn't allow you to do things like a job, stay longer than 90 days, or go to school. To do these things, you'll still need to apply for different cards.

Entry Not Guaranteed

Even if you have an ETIAS Visa, that doesn't mean you can get into the EU. It is not a permit to get in, but rather a permission to journey. Your ability to get in will rest on several things, like how you are traveling and what the border control officers decide.

Application Process and Cost

To get an ETIAS Visa, you have to fill out an application on the ETIAS page. The registration fee is about seven dollars or seven euros. During the application process, you will need to give a lot of personal information.

Passport Renewal Tip

If your passport is going to end the next year, you might want to renew it. By updating your passport and ETIAS Visa at the same time, you can travel worry-free for three years.

FAQs and Additional Information

On the official EU website, there are a lot of Frequently Asked Questions (FAQs) and useful facts about the ETIAS Visa. But keep in mind that as the system is put into place, some questions may still not be answered. Keep an eye out for new information and changes.

Starting in January 2024, travelers from countries like the US, UK, Canada, and others will need to meet the ETIAS Visa standard. Visit the official ETIAS website to make sure you have everything you need for a trip that goes smoothly and is fun.

Getting Around GALWAY

Walking is the best way to get around Galway. There are a lot of small streets and places where only people can walk, so it's easy to walk anywhere in the central business center. The city's bike-share scheme is another easy and cheap way to get around. But if you want to see the Cliffs of Moher or the Wild Atlantic Way on your own, you might want to rent a car.

If you'd rather let someone else drive, there are a lot of tour companies that offer packages that include sightseeing. We've included a few of these on our list of the best Ireland trips. Also, the Cliffs of Moher can be reached by Bus Éireann during the summer months. This is one of the city's more distant sights.

Shannon Airport (SNN), which is about 60 miles south of Galway, is the closest. From Shannon Airport to Galway, you can take Bus Éireann. Adult tickets start at 60 euros, which is about $72. At the airport, you can also rent cars from big companies like Hertz, Avis, and Europcar. Dublin Airport (DUB), which is about 130 miles east of Galway, is another choice.

Bus Éireann and a few other companies also run services between Dublin and Galway. Ireland West Airport Knock (NOC), which is about 60 miles north of Galway, is another choice, but it only has a few flights from London and Liverpool each day. You can rent a car or take Bus Éireann from Knock to Galway.

If you want a more beautiful way to get from Dublin to Galway, you could take the train, which takes about 2 1/2 hours. Irish Rail has many trips every day. When you book online, adult tickets start at 16.99 euros, which is about $20.

Getting around On Foot (We walked)

The best way to see the city center is on foot since many streets are only for people on foot and it's easy to get to all of the major sights.

Bus

Bus Éireann runs buses in the city and all around it. Most of the routes start from Eyre Square, which is in the middle of town. Any trip in the city that is longer than 7 12 kilometers (4.6 miles) costs 2.70 euros, which is about $3.20. Any trip shorter than 7 kilometers costs 2.30 euros, which is about $2.70. If you buy a reloadable Leap Card, you'll get a 30% discount on your ticket. A Leap Card can be bought at many stations and stores.

Bike

Through a bike-share scheme sponsored by Coca-Cola Zero, you can borrow or rent one of 195 bikes at 16 stations all over the city. If you want to use a bike for less than 30 minutes, it's free, but even renting one for three days for 3 euros (about $3.50) is a good deal.

Car

You can rent a car at the airport or in the city center if you need one for day trips or exploring outside of the city. If you do take a car, don't forget that you have to drive on the left side of the road. The speed limits are given in kilometers per hour, so it's a good idea to learn how to convert or print out a chart. Most car rental companies want you to have a license from the country where you live, not a foreign one. Check with the rental company before you leave.

Taxi

If you need a taxi in town, it's easy to find one near hotels and other big sites. You can also use ride-hailing apps like FreeNow which are famous and easy to use in many cities. But keep in mind that these services may not be available in all places. For cab rides, it's always a good idea to have cash on hand, since not all taxis take credit cards.

Tips for using FreeNow in Galway:

- Download the FreeNow app and create an account.
- Enter your pickup and drop-off locations.
- Select the type of vehicle you want to hail.
- Pay for your ride using the app.

Public Transportation in GALWAY

You can get to Ireland and Galway faster than ever before, and you have more options for efficient transportation than you did in the past. Once you get there, it will be easy to get around.

Here, you can find information about how to get to and from Galway City, which is in the west of Ireland, by bus, train, boat, and plane. This part also has information about how to get around Galway.

1. Aran Bikes Hire

Aran Bike Hire is on Inis Mor Island and rents out high-quality bikes to people who come to the island. You can rent a wide range of bikes for the day or a whole vacation. When you get off the boat on Inis Mor Island, Aran Bike Hire is right at the beginning of the pier, so you don't have to walk for a long time to find a bike. You will also get a free map of Inis Mor that shows both the well-known and less well-known treasures on the island. Since Inis Mor island is small, the best way to see it is by bike.

2. Aer Aran Islands

Aer Aran Islands is a small airline that offers daily flights to the three Aran Islands and scenic flights in the area. Connemara Regional Airport is in Inverin, which is 27 km from Galway City and close to the Rossaveal boat port. This is where flights leave from. During the busy season, there are planes every hour, and they only last about 10 minutes. The prices are fair, and the trip will stay with you forever.

From Connemara Airport, scenic flights fly southeast to the Cliffs of Moher, following the coast of Co Clare. The trip then goes north-west along Galway Bay, where you can see the three Aran Islands and get a great view of Dun Aengus Fort on Inis Mór, Inis Oirr, and Inis Meain before heading back to Connemara Airport.

3. All Things Connemara

They are called "All Things Connemara," and they are mostly a store that sells goods, services, and activities that show off and support the beautiful history and community of Connemara. When we say "heritage," It means the Past, Present, and Future.

Five important areas in this main store:

Products: Crafts, textiles, and other goods made or made in Connemara, with an e-commerce site.

Taste will show off the wide range of local foods they have, from seafood to plate, by highlighting restaurants, chefs, and goods.

Businesses – An informative list of Connemara's most important businesses, organizations, and groups.

By renting hybrid and pedal-assisted electric bikes, i.e makes cycling easier and more available for everyone.

Events: With some new ideas,its also a place where you can find out about all the activities and events in the area.

4. Aran Island Ferries

All year long, Aran Island Ferries take people to the Aran Islands, which are in Galway Bay. Both Galway City Docks and Ros a' Mhl, a port 23 miles west of Galway City center, have services that leave every day. In June 2021, the new service between Galway City and Aran began.

Every day at 9:30 a.m., trains leave for Galway City. There are two trips a day from Rossaveel to Inis Mór. Here are the schedules for ferries.

Aran Island Boats run a fleet of high-end, purpose-built boats with different passenger capacities to handle both private charters and regular sailings and to make sure that their customers get the best service possible. Except for the Sea Sprinter, their boats have a snack bar with light food and alcoholic drinks.

Travelers from Rossaveel should take one hour to drive from the city to the port, and they must check in 45 minutes before their ship leaves.

Senior Smart Pass and Irish Free Travel Pass can be used.

Questions People Usually Ask

Is there a place to park at Galway Harbour?

Yes, you can park your car at Galway Harbour, which is right next to the door to the Harbour Hotel parking lot.

Where do I go to get on the boat to Galway City?

All customers must pick up their tickets from offices in Galway, which are at 37–39 Forster Street or 1 Victoria Place. Then walk for 15 minutes to Galway Harbour (Eircode: H91 E9PR) to catch the boat.

When can we get on?

Everyone should be ready to board the plane 30 minutes before it leaves.

Can you bring your dog on the ferry?

Dogs are allowed on the boat, but they have to be on a leash on the outside deck for the whole trip.

Can I bring my own bike on the boat with me?

Yes, there are some spots for bikes on the ferry, but you should reserve your spot when you buy your boat ticket. The cost to move a normal or electric bike back and forth is €20.00 (€10.00 one way).

Are there still boats leaving from Rossaveel?

Yes, as usual, boats leave from Rossaveel Ferry Terminal

5. Big O Taxi

Big O Taxis has over 210 drivers and a fleet of more than 180 new cars. It has grown quickly to become Galway's largest and most efficient taxi business. Putting money into its future by getting a new computer system. GPS can be used to keep track of each car.

6. Rent a bike in Ireland

Galway's No.1 Bike Hire Company is your one-stop shop for all your riding needs. they offer a wide range of hire services, including day bike hire, self-guided tours, guided tours, and long- or short-term student bike hire. Mountain Trail Bike Shop on Middle Street is right in the middle of Galway's city center.

7. Budget Car Rental

Budget Car Rental Ireland has the friendliest service in Ireland and the best deals for car rentals. As well as the big towns, you can rent in Dublin, Shannon, Cork, Knock, and Belfast.

8. Irish Bus (Bus Éireann)

Bus Éireann has many different bus and train services for different types of customers and markets.

Expressway Inter-Urban provides bus routes. Commuter bus services start in Dublin, Cork, Limerick, Galway, and Waterford and go out in all directions. Services for city buses in Cork, Galway, Limerick, and Waterford. Town Services – In Athlone, Balbriggan, Drogheda, Dundalk, Navan, and Sligo.

Expressway for Bus Éireann

Expressway provides daily, high-quality bus service from Galway to places all over Ireland, such as Cork, Limerick, Ballina, Derry, and more. There is free WiFi, a place to charge your phone, and leather seats that can be leaned back.

9. Irish Campervans

The best company in Ireland to rent a motorhome from, with great prices, customer service, and availability. Celtic Campervans is the self-drive campervan holiday expert, and their modern motorhomes let you travel all over Ireland and enjoy your vacation your way.

10. City Taxis Galway

City Taxis is a reputable taxi company that offers services like airport transfers, luxury taxis, and tours of the city and Connemara. With their easy-to-remember phone number, +353 91 52 52 52, you can easily call a taxi in Galway whenever you need to get somewhere.

11. Citylink

Citylink has many trips back and forth between Galway and Dublin, Limerick, Cork, and Clifden. Fair prices, travel times that take as little time as possible, and new coaches that make the trip safe and enjoyable.

Ticketing and Transport Passes in GALWAY

In Galway, Ireland, there are many different kinds of tickets and passes that can be used for public transportation. Here's a quick look at a few of the most popular choices:

- **Galway City Pass**: For 24 or 48 hours, this pass lets you use Galway City's public transportation as much as you want. It also gives you savings on things like the Galway City Museum, the ferry to the Aran Islands, and the Galway Cathedral.
- **CityLink** is a bus service that connects Galway City and the areas around it. They have many kinds of tickets, such as single prices, day passes, and weekly passes.
- **Bus Éireann:** Bus Éireann is Ireland's main bus company. They have a variety of lines to and from Galway, as well as routes within the city. You can buy single rides, day passes or passes for a whole week.
- **TFI Leap Card**: The TFI Leap Card is a smart card that can be reloaded and used on all buses and trains in Galway. Any Leap Top-Up Agent can sell you a Leap Card, and any Leap Top-Up Agent can also add money to your Leap Card.

Which ticket or pass is best for you will depend on what you need and how you plan to travel. The Galway City Pass is a good choice if you are going to stay in Galway City and use public transportation a lot. If you want to go to other places in the area, CityLink or Bus Éireann might be a better choice.

And if you plan to use public transportation for a long time, the TFI Leap Card might be the most cost-effective choice.

Tips on how to buy tickets and use Galway's public transportation:

- You can buy tickets and transportation passes for all of the above things online or at several places in Galway City.
- If you want to buy a one-way ticket, make sure you have the exact amount of cash because bus drivers usually don't have change.
- Make sure to tag on and tag off at the beginning and end of each trip if you are using a Leap Card.
- If you're not sure which ticket or pass you need or if you have any questions about how to use public transportation in Galway, feel free to ask a bus driver or another staff member for help.

Transportation Tips

Galway is a somewhat small city that is simple to navigate on foot or by bicycle. Buses, taxis, and private rental cars are just a few of the public transit choices that are offered.

Biking and walking: These are two excellent methods to get around Galway. There are many pedestrian-friendly streets in the relatively small city center. Additionally, there are many bike lanes, and there are several stores in the city where you may hire a bike.

Several bus lines are run by Galway Bus Éireann around the city and its surroundings. If you are staying in a more rural area or if you have a lot of luggage, taking the bus is a good way to move around.

Taxis: Although they might be pricey, taxis are a convenient method to move around Galway. Taxis have meters, and the cost varies according to how far you go.

Private hire vehicles: If you are traveling in a party or require a vehicle with additional luggage room, private hire vehicles, like those run by FreeNow, are a fantastic alternative for moving around Galway. Although the fee may be a little bit more expensive than a taxi rate, private rental vehicles are also metered.

Tips

- You may simply travel by foot or bicycle if you are staying in the city center.
- You might want to take a bus or taxi if you are staying in a more rural area.
- You might want to think about choosing a private hire vehicle if you're going in a group or if you require a vehicle with additional luggage capacity.
- Be warned that private hire cars and taxis are quite pricey, especially during rush hour.
- Make sure you buy a Leap Card if you intend to use the public transit system. Reusable prepaid cards called Leap Cards are accepted on Galway's buses and trains.

Omey Island

CHAPTER FOUR

Best Beaches in GALWAY

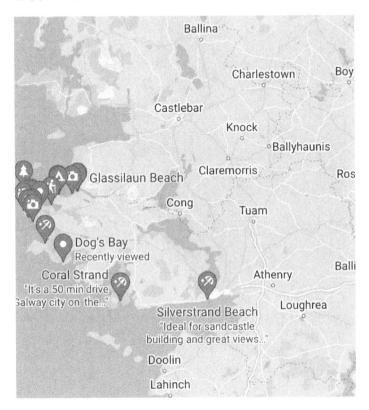

The city of Galway is very desirable because it has many beautiful beaches nearby. Some of the best beaches on the west coast of Ireland are in Galway County. Salthill has the closest beach to Galway. It's just a short walk along the walkway that starts in The Claddagh area from the city center. In Salthill, three different beaches are very popular with both tourists and locals during the summer.

Some locals even swim in the winter when the weather isn't as nice. People who like to swim love the diving board at Blackrock, which is at the end of the Salthill promenade. Brave people dare to test their skills against the rough Atlantic sea.

From May to September, lifeguards watch over Salthill Beach and most of the other bigger beaches in the county. Here are some of Galway's great beaches:

Dog's Bay / Gurteen Bay Beaches, Roundstone

These are two of the most beautiful beaches in County Galway and probably all of Western Ireland. They are right next to each other. They are only two miles from the pretty town of Roundstone in Connemara, Co. Galway.

One of the best stretches of coastline in Connemara is made up of Dogs Bay and Gurteen Bay. From there, you can see Errisbeg and the farmland around it. This is Dogs Bay. It is a beautiful horseshoe-shaped bay with a white sand beach that is more than a mile long.

Like Gurteen Bay, the sand isn't made of normal limestone. Instead, it's made up of pieces of seashells that give it a clear white color.

Both beaches are safe for swimming and other water sports like sailing and kitesurfing because they are well protected from currents. They are also great places to go for a walk.

Glassilaun Beach, North Connemara

You'd think that beaches like Glassilaun would only be found in faraway, warm places. Most people who visit Connemara are surprised to find that Ireland has beaches that are so stunningly beautiful. With beautiful mountains to the north and east and a location between the bays of Renvyle and Killary, this spot has some of the most beautiful scenery in the world.

From a small parking lot in the back, you can get to the crescent-shaped white sand beach through sand dunes. The water is very clear, and the beach gradually slopes down to make it safe and fun to swim. A small island is at the western end of the beach. It can be reached at low tide or explored by raft or kayak.

Lettergesh Beach

If it's hot, you shouldn't go to the Caribbean. Instead, you should go to Lettergesh Beach on Ireland's beautiful west coast. The beach here is one of the nicest in Galway, and you should go for a walk there even if the weather is bad. Lettergesh Beach is in the beautiful Connemara area of County Galway.

This place is on the Renvyle Peninsula, about an hour and a half's drive from Galway City. Clifden is also only thirty minutes away by car.

Lettergesh Beach looks like it belongs on a postcard. There are beautiful golden dunes and the Atlantic Ocean, which is very clear. In the background, Mweerlea

Mountain stands tall. It's the best place to relax on a nice day, on the golden sands, and in the wide open space.

Often, you might be the only person on the beach. The sounds of the sea and birds singing are very different from the background of sheep grazing in the green hills and mountains. This beach is well-sheltered, and the calm, blue water is very appealing. A lot of people like to swim here all year. But it's important to know that the beach doesn't have any lifeguards on duty.

There is a large parking lot at Lettergesh Beach, but people in wheelchairs or who have trouble moving around may have trouble getting to the sand because they have to walk across a field of stones.

Trá an Dóilín Coral Beach, Carraroe

The area around Carraroe Coral Strand, which is also called Trá a Dóilin, is very beautiful. The beach is known for having very fine coral. During the swimming season, the beach has lifeguards and bathrooms. The beach is generally less crowded than city beaches and has lots of small rock pools to explore. It's also a good place to snorkel.

Salthill Beach

Along the famous Salthill Promenade, the beach at Salthill is made up of several smaller beaches that are divided by rocks. The beach goes all the way down to Blackrock Diving Tower, which is at the western end. Different beaches have different types of sand and rocks.

Ladies Beach is the biggest and busiest. It has its beach hut where you can get coffee, ice cream, and treats. It is in Galway City and has a view of Galway Bay, which is a Special Area of Conservation. Beach lifeguards are on duty from mid-May to the end of September, from 11 a.m. to 7 p.m. Salthill Beach has a blue flag and is a huge hit when the weather is nice in the summer.

White Strand Beach, Renvyle, Co. Galway

White Strand is a lovely beach in Renvyle. It has 1 km of fine white sand, water that is as clear as glass, and amazing views of the Mweelrea mountains in South Mayo. The beach is split in half by a small hill that gives you a great view of the whole beach. A short country road leads to the beach. It is just past the Renvyle Beach Caravan and Camping Park, which has a small parking lot and is marked with signs.

Kilmurvey Beach, Inis Mór

A blue flag beach, Kilmurvey Beach is a beautiful sandy beach on Inis Mor, the biggest of the Aran Islands. No matter what age, you can swim there safely because there aren't any strong currents like there are at some of the more secret and hard to get to beaches. On a sunny day, the blue water looks stunning next to the white sand. On the sands, there are great places to have a picnic, and there are bathrooms close to the roads. You can jump off the old pier into the clear water when the tide is right.

Spiddal Beach, An Spidéal

The wide sandy beach at An Spidéal runs along the promenade and is framed by rocky outcroppings on either side. It's a great choice for beach fans. The water consistently gets a blue flag for good quality. The depth of the water rises slowly so that people of all ages can swim safely, and there is a lifeguard hut there from May to September. You can easily park along the promenade, which makes it easy to take all your beach gear to your favorite spot. There are also many shops and restaurants nearby to meet all your needs. Just across the street is the beautiful Ceardlann Craft Village, which you should check out. To end a great day at the beach, watch the sun go down over Galway Bay.

Dumhnach Beach, Inishbofin Island

To the east of Inishbofin Island is Dumhach Beach, which is about a 15-minute walk from the harbor. At the southern end of the beach, there is a long rocky outcrop that protects it from the waves. This outcrop links Inishbofin Island to its smaller neighbor, Inishlyon Island.

Its calm seas and long, clean, white sand beach backed by small sand dunes make it a beautiful place to swim on sunny days. The Green Coast Award for environmental achievement was given to Dumhnach Beach.

Where to stay in GALWAY: Best Areas and Neighborhoods

Galway is a city in West Ireland. It is in the province of Connacht and the county of Galway. It's the middle point of the Wild Atlantic Way, which is one of the most beautiful drives in the world. This small Irish city has a lot of history, beautiful scenery, and a cozy feel, so it's no surprise that artists and singers have been drawn there for hundreds of years.

Galway is a great place to see traditional Ireland because it is full of cozy pubs, small shops, and great restaurants.

Where to stay in Galway?

Galway City Center, Salthill, Oranmore, The Claddagh, Kinvara, and The Docks are the best places for tourists and first-timers to stay. These are some of the city's most popular and safest areas, with lots of things to do and places to stay.

Galway is a pretty small city, so if you want to stay in the city itself, don't worry too much about which neighborhood you choose. The main places are all close enough to walk between them.

You can choose to stay in the Galway City Center, one of the major towns like Salthill, Clifden, Oranmore, or one of many smaller villages.

If you do decide to stay farther away, there is a good bus network that will get you around. It will be easy to get around the area, even if you choose to stay in one of the nearby towns.

Don't forget that Galway is in the Republic of Ireland, not Northern Ireland. This means that the local currency is the euro, not the pound. If you're going to bring cash, make sure you get the right stuff.

THE BEST PLACES FOR TOURISTS TO STAY IN GALWAY ARE:

1. The Center of Galway

The Galway City Centre is the best place to stay in Galway for first-time visitors because it is in the best spot. You'll be right in the middle of everything if you stay here. Top tourist spots, as well as many restaurants, bars, and shops, are all within walking distance.

Galway city center is the busy center of the region's name-giving town. You can spend your vacation in the city center if you want a faster-paced trip with lots to see and do. Tourists who want to enjoy a lively evening, great shopping, easy access to public transportation, and a truly Irish atmosphere love staying in Galway City Centre.

There are a lot of restaurants and bars in the city center, just like in any other city center. If you want a snack in between, you can go to one of the many bakeries, dessert shops, or food stands in the area.

Any Irish city would be incomplete without a good number of pubs and bars, so you will have no trouble finding something to do the night. Also, the bars are great spots to meet people from the area and have conversations with interesting people.

Additionally, if you'd rather go to bars for fun in the evening, most of Galway's can be found in the city center. The Latin Quarter and Eyre Square are where most of them are.

In Galway, Eyre Square, which is also called John F. Kennedy Park, is where all the fun events happen. The green park is a great place to relax in the summer, but it's a great place to meet up all year round.

There is a Christmas market in the square every winter. At the same time, different works and shows appear here all year long.

One of the most famous sights in Galway is the Quincentennial Fountain in Eyre Square, which has copper sails. The waterfall was put in place to mark the 500th anniversary of Galway becoming a city. The sails show that the city has a seafaring history.

It is just across the street from Eyre Square and in the direction of the Latin Quarter. The remembrance is made up of a copy of a wall from the home of Mayor James Lynch in the 1400s.

After his son was found guilty of murder, the mayor had to hang him. Some say that the window at the top of the tribute is the same window from which the hanging happened so many years ago.

The most famous and impressive building in Galway isn't very old, even though the city has a lot of history. Galway Cathedral is a beautiful, gray brick building that towers over the area. It didn't open until 1965.

Galway Cathedral stands out against the city skyline. It is built on the site of the old city prison, which is just across the Salmon Weir Bridge. From the outside, the church is beautiful, with its wide dome, tall twin towers, and bright stained glass.

The inside of the church is also very beautiful. The exposed gray brick gives the vaulted hall a stylish and classy look, giving it a more modern take on the busy opulence of older churches.

The 14th-century Saint Nicholas' Collegiate Church is another important place of worship in the middle of Galway's life. It is the biggest medieval parish church in Ireland. It is the site of many interesting statues and memorials, such as the Jane Eyre, James Kearney, and Adam Bures pieces in Galway.

You can also walk along the Lough Atalia path to see the beautiful Lough Atalia Lake, which is a large estuary lagoon to the east of Galway City.

The Eyre Square Shopping Centre is in the main shopping areas on William Street and Shop Street. If you like to shop, go there. With more than 70 shops from across the country and the UK, Eyre Square Shopping Centre is the liveliest spot in the city.

To get food and Irish beer, go down Quay Street. It has some of the city's best pubs and restaurants.

There are good public transportation connections in the city center, with Galway Train Station and Galway Coach Station nearby. These make it easy to get to other parts of the city and to see the Cliffs of Moher, Kinsale, and Cork.

In the city center of Galway, there are a lot of different places to stay at a wide range of prices. On this street, you can find some of the city's most expensive and least expensive restaurants. Surprisingly, the city center is a great place to stay in Galway on a budget. There are cute, cheap hostels right next to nicer, more expensive hotels.

2. Salthill

Salthill is a lively beach vacation town that is only a short bus ride from Galway City to the west. So close to each other that it's simple to think that Salthill is just another neighborhood in the bigger town.

Salthill is a famous summer vacation spot because it has a long stretch of white-sand beaches that are both sandy and pebbly. You can have the best of both worlds on your trip—a city break and a laid-back holiday. Tourists from all over the world come to the area to enjoy the rare Irish sun.

Staying here would be especially good for families with kids. There are many family-friendly activities and sites close by, as well as open spaces for kids to play and the city's sights that are only a short drive away. Salthill has a lot of useful features.

You can take a nice walk along the Salthill Promenade when you're not lying on the beach. At Blackrock Point, the end of Salthill Prom, you can take part in a strange local custom and enjoy beautiful views of Galway Bay.

Someone may have put up a sign at the end of the walk telling you to "kick the wall." It's not clear where the custom came from, but for years, people from all over the world have been kicking the wall for good luck.

You can now give a coin to charity in exchange for your good luck kick. A collection box has been put up against the wall. Some people like to relax at Blackrock Tower, which is on Blackrock Point.

Blackrock Tower is made up of a rocky path that goes out into the water and finishes at a public diving platform. People are strong enough to jump off the board into the cold water at any time of the year, but summer is when everybody does it the most.

The Galway Aquarium, which is also known as the National Aquarium of Ireland, is one of the most popular places for tourists to visit in Salthill. The aquarium is mostly about animals that are native to Ireland, but it also has many other kinds and educational displays.

There are some very interesting displays at the aquarium that center on conservation and biodiversity. The Galway Atlantaquaria is a great place for a family day out because it has things for people of all kinds to enjoy.

People who like to play golf will also enjoy Salthill. One of the best golf grounds in the country, Galway Golf Club, is there.

As a famous vacation spot, the town has a lot of places to stay, especially along the beach. Several self-catering flats look out over the water. Further inland, there are several guesthouses and bed and breakfasts.

During the busy summer months, Salthill is not the cheapest place to stay in the City of the Tribes. Many of them are cheaper, though, especially those farther from the water.

3. Oranmore

The Burren, Connemara, the Aran Islands, Galway City, and the Corrib and Lough Mask water systems are all easy to get to from Oranmore.

Oranmore is from the Middle Ages, and many of the houses there are still the same as they were back then. The historic town is beautiful, and the best place to stay if you want to be close to cute stone houses and thatched cottages, especially along Main Street.

The city is only a short drive away, and Oranmore is a cute, easygoing place to stay while you explore the rest of the town. You can take a bus to get to the city center in thirty minutes if you don't have a car with you.

There are, of course, lots of things to do in and around the town. There are so many great places in Oranmore that it's hard to believe it's only a small area. There are also lots of cozy bars where you can meet people from the area.

Galway Bay is on the fourth side of Oranmore, and the beautiful scenery is on the other three. Many chances will be given for you to walk around in the fresh air and enjoy the beautiful scenery. There is a lot more to find outside of town for people who want to go look around.

Oranmore Castle is the main thing to see in Oranmore. The square tower looks out over Galway Bay and is right on the water. It's hard to say for sure, but records suggest it was made around the 1400s.

Even though the castle is a private home, it is often open to the public for tours and viewings, especially in the summer. You should still go there even when it's not open to enjoy its beautiful front and the way it stands out against the skyline.

If you have time to go outside of Oranmore, there are, of course, many more castles to find.

Outside of the town, Enville Castle and Ardfry Castle are both only a few miles away. If you like taking walks in the country, it would be nice to spend the afternoon walking through the fields or along the beach to one or both of them.

Even though Oranmore is a long way from the city center, the prices for places to stay aren't that different from those in the city center. Although it's not too expensive, it's not the best choice if you don't want to give up a central spot for cheap prices.

4. Kinvara

A bus goes from the cute little seaside town of Kinvara to Galway Center, which is about twenty miles south around the bay from Galway City. Kinvara is a great place to stop on any coastal road trip. It is on the N67 road, which runs along the coast from Galway City all the way south to County Kerry.

Kinvara is home to less than 2,000 people. So, if you want to feel like you're in a small town, this is a great choice. The port area is the busy part of town. From there, you can watch the fishing boats move around on the water.

People from the area get together at the weekly farmer's market on the main road every Friday. It's a great chance to buy crafts and other items made in the area as gifts. When you get hungry, you can also try a lot of fresh food, as well as local meals and home-baked goods.

And even though the town is very small, there are many places to pick from. You won't go hungry in Kinvara, whether you want fresh seafood with a view of the harbor, traditional Irish food in a cozy bar, or stylish Italian food.

There are many clubs and bars, like Green's Bar, where you can spend the evening after dinner, especially along the main road. In the summer, it's nice to sit outside at a bar or restaurant by the water and enjoy the view and the breeze from the water.

Kinvara is surrounded by beautiful nature. Kinvara is perfect for people who love being outside and walking through endless fields. It's easy to see why Ireland is called "The Emerald Isle" in places like this.

Along with Kinvara Harbour, Dunguaire Castle is one of the most important places to see in Kinvara. The Dungaire Castle, which was built in the 1600s, is right on the bay and looks out over the water. Over the years, the castle has been in many movies, books, and stories. In addition to tours, people can also enjoy the many banquets that are held in the castle rooms.

Because the town is so small, there aren't many places to stay. In line with the cozy feel of the area, most of the guesthouses and bed & breakfasts will be run by families. One of the best places to stay in all of West Ireland is here.

5. The Claddagh

The Claddagh is a cool area of town that is just across the River Corrib from the city center. The Claddagh is also a bridge that makes it easy to get from the city center to Salthill. The Claddagh is a great place to stay if you can't decide between a city break and a relaxing beach holiday.

An area mostly made up of homes, it is just far enough from the busy center to keep a more relaxed vibe. Despite that, it still makes it easy to get to the main town's sights and sites.

This is also a great place for families with kids because it is quieter, there are open parks, and it's easy to get to Galway's major attractions. You won't lose your kids in a crowd because there is room for them to run around.

The Claddagh is still known as the largest fishing town in Ireland, even though it has become part of a bigger city. Open parks, like South Park and Celia Griffin Memorial Park, line the shore. These are great places to relax and enjoy the view of the ocean.

It's also where the custom of the Claddagh ring came from. All over the world, the Claddagh ring is seen as a sign of love and friendship. This link was made in Claddagh in the 1700s and makes the town a popular place for couples to go on love getaways today.

Claddagh doesn't have as many bars and restaurants because it's mostly private. Most of what's there is in the north, near the Wolfe Tone Bridge. Things are fine with that, though.

In the nearby places, many restaurants are only a short walk away. After a busy night out, you can come home to the peace and quiet of this less busy neighborhood.

Several types of lodging are offered in the area that fit with the calm atmosphere. Rather than staying in a big hotel, you can stay in a cozy hostel or bed & breakfast run by a family. In general, the prices are also reasonable.

6. The Docks

If you want to see beautiful views of Galway Bay, the Docks area should be at the top of your list. The Docks have views of the water in almost every direction because they are right where the River Corrib flows into the bay.

One of the best things about the Docks is that it is right in the middle of Galway. You will be able to walk to many of the city's sites, as well as some that are closer to the water.

A boat tour along the River Corrib starts at the busy Port of Galway. This is a great thing to do on a nice day. You could also rent your own boat and go out into the bay. If you'd rather enjoy the view from land, for lunch or dinner, go to one of the bars or restaurants that look out over the harbor.

Along Lough Corrib, the well-known Long Walk is a nice place to walk with its houses, boats, and small harbor. It has beautiful views of the water and the Claddagh.

You can start the Long Walk at the Galway City Museum. You should go there if you want to learn about how the area has changed over time and about people from the past and present.

Artifacts and relics from Galway's past and up to the present day are on display at the city museum. Before it was moved to its present, dedicated location, it was kept in the Spanish Arch.

The Spanish Arch is a stone doorway that is one of the few parts of the old Galway city wall that still stands. It was first called "Ceann a Bhalla," but many years after it was built, it was called the "Spanish Arch."

No one knows for sure how it got its name, but it's likely because the arch was the main way for Spanish merchants to enter the city. The arch is also not far from Galway's Latin Quarter.

The Latin Quarter is full of restaurants and bars. It has a Mediterranean feel that you wouldn't expect to find in the middle of an Irish town.

There are tapas bars, Italian restaurants, and fresh seafood places here that serve tasty food. In the summer, it's especially nice because you can sit outside on the streetside decks and feel like you're in the Mediterranean.

There is a Hall Of The Red Earl that people who are interested in the past of the city should see. The stone foundations of the hall were dug up in the late 1990s. They are the remains of one of Galway's oldest buildings, which dates back to the city's beginning in the 1300s.

The spot is now protected by glass, and people can look at it from a raised platform. Around the small museum are relics that have been found and copies of similar items that show how people lived in medieval Galway.

In the Docks area, there are some beautiful, high-quality, small hotels. There aren't as many cheap choices here as there are in the city center, but the ones that are here feel a bit more high-end and exclusive.

7. National University of Ireland Galway (NUIG) Area

Younger tourists love the area around the National University of Ireland Galway, which is tucked into a bend in the River Corrib. This area has a much calmer vibe and is very conveniently located close to the city center.

This is one of the more beautiful neighborhoods in the city center. It has a lot of public parks and green places, as well as a long stretch of river. You have a lot of room to spread out and relax, and you can always walk a short distance to some interesting places to visit.

Terryland Castle is just across the water. The castle from the 1600s is mostly destroyed now, but it has a cool view of the water and is fun to explore up close.

One of the best things about the place is the university itself. Some of the most famous sights in Galway are the building's beautiful cloisters and large stone front. Everyone is welcome to look around the whole campus, so you should make time to stop by.

Along with the usual college town attractions, there are some interesting sites to check out in this area.

It's only a short walk across the street to the James Mitchell Geology Museum. There is a great collection of fossils and rare stones in the museum that you should check out.

The Cúirt Literary Trail also starts at the university's Quadrangle, which fits with the area's academic feel.

After going south to the river, the trail keeps going along the coast. Along the path, there are signs with short passages from different works of literature by Galwegians.

The neighborhood is popular with younger tourists, but it's not one of the cheapest places to stay in the city. The university area is definitely in the middle range, and there are some beautiful, stylish places to stay. But it's not the place to look for cheap things.

8. Newcastle

The residential area of Newcastle is on the northern edge of the city. It's much quieter, less crowded, and less touristy about a mile outside of the city center. You can still walk or take the bus into the city whenever you want, and when you're done exploring, you can go back to your peaceful oasis.

There may not be as many places to stay because the area is more private, but the ones that are there are usually cheaper than places that are more popular with tourists. This doesn't just apply to places to stay. There is also no tourist tax on the area's bars, pubs, and restaurants.

The beautiful scenery around Galway is much easier to get to from Newcastle, which is another reason to stay there. To get to Lough Corrib, just follow the River Corrib north through lush green fields.

The Republic of Ireland's biggest lake is Lough Corrib. The land around the lake is now a protected area and has beautiful hiking trails. Newcastle is a great place to live if you like being outside and enjoying nature.

If you're not quite up for a full-on hike, you can take it easy and walk along the river to Menlo Castle instead. To get to the 16th-century castle, which is now broken down and covered in ivy, you will have to cross the river by Terryland Castle and then head north.

The bones of the old house are open to everyone, so feel free to look around. On warmer days, it's a great place to have lunch because it's right next to the river.

There is a silly house called the Martin Tea-House Folly just across the river from Menlo Castle. The teahouse was built in the 1800s so that the landowners could enjoy views of the river. It is now a cute spot for people going along the south bank of the river.

9. Clifden

Clifden is a lively coastal town in the west of County Galway. It is in the heart of the beautiful Connemara area, at the base of Twelve Pins Mountain. Clifden is about fifty miles from Galway City. It's not the best place for first-time guests to the area, but it's a great place to stop on a road trip along the coast.

Even though the town is very small, there is a lot in it. You can look around in a lot of small shops, museums, and art galleries. There are also many great restaurants in the area and a good number of sights to see. Dog's Bay Beach and Connemara National Park are also close by.

You can spend the nights in one of the many pubs or bars and enjoy lively Irish entertainment. Go to one of the cozy bars if you'd rather have a quiet night. If you'd rather have a louder night out, there are a lot of bars and places with live music in the area.

I think you should spend an evening at Lowry's Music & Whiskey Bar. Some things are more Irish than others, like whiskey. To get into the spirit of things traditionally Irish, try some local beers and listen to traditional music in a cozy Irish bar.

Clifden Castle is the most famous place to visit in the area. The lovely residential house was built in 1818 as the home of John D'Arcy, who founded Clifden. It is now in bad shape. With its many crenelated turrets standing among the crumbling stone walls, it still makes a beautiful picture against the scenery.

The pretty castle gate, which is part of what's left of the old castle wall, leads to Clifden Castle. The castle is about a mile west of the town of Clifden. It's a nice walk along country roads, or you can drive there in no time.

As you walk along the coast, you'll see many more places and monuments to explore. The John D'Arcy Monument is right next to the path that leads to Clifden Castle. The Alcock and Brown Memorial is on the other side of the bay, about a mile away.

The sunsets from the tops of the hills here are especially beautiful because they are close to the western coast of Ireland. It is well worth the trouble to hike out to them along one of the many beach trails. You can always drive up to see the view if you don't want to walk.

From Galway, you can take a normal bus to get to Clifden. You can also take the N59 straight from Galway to Clifden, going through Oughterard, Maam Cross, and Recess.

Even though it's a pretty small area and not the most popular tourist spot in the area, there are still a lot of places to stay. A wide range of holiday homes, bed and breakfasts, and family-run guesthouses are available at different price points.

Best Luxury Hotels

Lots of fun, history, and culture Galway is one of the most popular places to visit in Ireland. It could be the Latin Quarter's clubs and bars. It could be the city's Gaelic roots and past, or it could be its beautiful location on the coast. Galway has a lot of beautiful places to fall in love with, like the Spanish Arch and Menlo Castle.

In the busy medieval Latin Quarter, you can go to traditional bars and order fish straight from the Atlantic while listening to live music. Some of the best restaurants in Galway are in small, cozy hotels. You can have afternoon tea with a view of Lough Atalia or dinner with award-winning local cooks serving fresh Galway crab and prime Galway beef.

Galway is the starting point for the Wild Atlantic Way and has a view of the wild western coast of Ireland. You can take fun day trips from Galway to the Aran Islands, Connemara National Park, the Cliffs of Moher, and The Burren, all of which are close to where you stay.

You'll want a nice hotel room to relax in after a long day of seeing and doing. Galway is lucky because it is full of old hotels, country manors, and fancy boutique hotels. There are so many that it might be hard to pick the right one.

Glenlo Abbey Hotel

Beautiful place, Very cute, Comfortable rooms. A favorite among lovers. The 5-star Glenlo Abbey Hotel & Estate is only 2 miles from the center of Galway. It has free parking, a golf course, and views of Lough Corrib and the dramatic West of Ireland scenery.

The 138-acre golf course is next to a lake and has a 21-bay driving range and golf classes. The Glenlo Abbey Hotel & Estate rooms all have a flat-screen TV, a marble bathroom with a power shower, free Wi-Fi, high-end toiletries, towels and slippers, and a marble bathroom.

You can also do falconry, shooting, and fishing on-site. Residents of the hotel can use the estate bicycles for free to go for a ride around Glenlo Abbey Estate. At the Glenlo Abbey Hotel & Estate, the Pullman Restaurant on the Orient Express is a one-of-a-kind place to eat, and they serve afternoon tea every day.

These antique Pullman train cars have been turned into restaurants while keeping their original look. They have two dining rooms. Palmers Bar & Kitchen is in the main hotel and is a great place for casual eating. It has a wide range of food options, a lively atmosphere, and cozy rooms. The River Room Restaurant has a beautiful setting.

Park House Hotel

Beautiful and classy, Great place to be. The Park House Hotel is in the middle of Galway and has all the comforts of a 4-star hotel with the kindness and personality of a boutique hotel. It has a kitchen that has won awards and rooms that are air-conditioned and have free Wi-Fi. The rooms are designed with soft colors, furniture made of natural wood, and high-end fabrics.

The award-winning Boss Doyle's Bar is another place where guests can relax. It has hand-carved oak-paneled ceilings, stained glass windows, and mood lighting. They have TVs with movie and sports programs, safes for laptops, and places to make tea and coffee. The table d'hôte menu at The Park Restaurant has tasty home-cooked food.

It uses high-quality local food, and there is a long list of wines to go with the food. Not far away are Galway Train Station and Eyre Square. The hotel is right next to a tourist office where guests can plan trips to the Aran Islands, Connemara, or the Cliffs of Moher.

The G Hotel

In style, Not like any other, Nice, soft beds. A favorite among lovers. G, I like the way you look! After spending a million euros to update its lobby, signature lounges, restaurant, and drink bar, Galway's g Hotel has become even more stylish. It is now the most stylish hotel in the western part of Ireland. The five-star luxury resort on the edge of Lough Atalia has a fresh new look thanks to Choice Hotel Group Ireland.

The ground-floor rooms are very different from one another, giving each one its unique personality. A warm and relaxing atmosphere is created by a range of soft taupes, grays, and plum-colored hints in high-end leather textured fabrics. These can be used for afternoon tea or a drink before dinner. The two other Signature Lounges in the hotel have been renovated to still feel glamorous and high-class but with a more understated touch.

The G Hotel has always been a place where people interested in fashion and design like to hang out. It opened in 2005 with a lot of fanfare for its famous designer, Phillip Tracey. The g brand has always been bold and different, using dark and light, bright colors, large mirrors and reflective lighting, and loud artwork and images that pay homage to the supermodels of the time. Together, these elements have created an iconic brand that tries to never be ordinary.

The idea behind the €1 million renovation was to take ideas from the experimental, the unusual, and the luxurious, and to give each of the hotel's famous signature rooms a unique look that praised individuality. It is known for its natural light, high ceilings, views of Lough Atalia, and the custom mirrored lighting installation by lighting artist Tom Dixon that gets a lot of photos. The design team at GW Design wanted to keep the big salon's stylish and classy vibe and give the room a sense of subtle sophistication.

The view of the Lough and the lighting installation are reflected in a new drink bar that looks like a jewel and has a dramatic back bar display made of mirrors. The restaurant at the g Hotel has been changed to GEO and has gone through the biggest changes of all the renovations.

The restaurant and cocktail bar used to be two different rooms, but the design team took down the wall between them to make them feel more open and spacious. The GEO Restaurant has a new garden patio that connects to it. The fresh botanical theme continues inside the restaurant. There is now a new drink bar in the middle of the open-plan room.

The walls are covered with a beautiful scene of flowers, ferns, palms, and leaves that draw people in. Statement chandeliers and smoked mirrors with an olive green color scheme and a faint sparkle draw the eye through the restaurant. Coral accents and lots of plants finish off the new GEO theme.

The blush pink velvets, tasseled chairs, and brass details in the Pink Room give it a high-class and mysterious look. The Blue Room, on the other hand, has a color scheme of ginger, charcoal, and rich wood. The leather, wood, and fabric wall paneling in this room make it a comfortable place to stay for a while.

The Dean Galway

Hip, Very cool, Nice, soft beds. A favorite among lovers. It opened in January 2022. There are free bikes, an outdoor pool, an exercise center, and a terrace at The Dean Galway in Galway. This 4-star hotel has free WiFi, room service, and a front desk that's open 24 hours a day.

At the bar, people can get something to drink. Each room has a desk, a flat-screen TV with satellite stations, a minibar, a kettle, a shower, and free toiletries. Each room has its own bathroom, hairdryer, and bed linens. There is a diner at the hotel that serves both American and Italian food.

You can also ask for vegetarian, dairy-free, or gluten-free choices. Eyre Square, Galway Railway Station, and Galway Greyhound Stadium are all popular places to visit near Dean Galway. Shannon Airport is the closest airport, which is 80 km away.

The Hardiman

Historic building. Beautiful land. Great place to be. Women like it. The rooms have a nice bed and a bathroom made of marble with high-end items. The rooms also have a press reader, free WiFi, and a flat-screen Chromecast TV. There is a train station and a bus stop right next to The Hardiman, which is in the middle of Galway. A five-minute walk will get you to the dock. The Gaslight Brasserie, the Oyster Bar, and the famous Parlour Lounge at The Hardiman are all on the lower ground floor. They are open every day and serve classic, tasty food. Guests can unwind in the Parlour Lounge, which has just been remodeled, or go for a walk in Galway City outside our door.

The Galmont Hotel & Spa

Very nice. Beautiful views. A favorite among lovers. The Galmont Hotel & Spa is only 200 meters from Eyre Square and has a view of Galway Bay. The restaurant has won awards, and the hotel also has the Spirit One Spa and Energize exercise and leisure. Egyptian cotton sheets and goose feather pillows are on big, fancy beds.

All of The Galmont Hotel & Spa's large rooms have free Wi-Fi and an LCD TV placed on the wall. There is a gym, a sauna, and a swimming pool at the spa center, and Elemis services are available.

There is an indoor pool and an exercise club at The Galmont, as well as a full-service spa. One of the hotel's two restaurants is open for business. There is a bar or lounge where people can relax with a drink. In public places, you can use the Internet wirelessly for free.

Food is served for breakfast and dinner at Marina's Restaurant. The Coopers Bar & Lounge has a patio with water views and serves food all day. This 4-star hotel has an office center on site. This hotel is good for the environment and has a spa, a sauna, and a pool for kids.

There is parking on-site (fee). It is not allowed to smoke at The Galmont. A 10-minute drive will get you to Galway Racecourse, which is only 55 miles from the hotel. The Galmont Hotel & Spa is only a 5-minute walk from Galway's city center.

Salthill Hotel

Women really like it. This classy hotel has a 25-meter pool, a spa, and a big gym. It has views of the famous Salthill Promenade, Galway Bay, and the Clare Hills. It is in the beautiful countryside of Galway, just 1 km from the city center. It is on the scenic road to Connemara National Park. All of the rooms at the Salthill Hotel have free WiFi, free tea and coffee, and flat-screen TVs with cable shows.

Each room has its bathroom with toiletries and a hair dryer. Some rooms also have lovely views of the sea. Every day, full Irish breakfasts are given. The Amber Room and Prom Restaurants offer a range of menus, all of which are made with food from nearby farms. There are many drinks to choose from at Blackrock Cafe and Bar, including wines, cocktails, and unique teas and coffees.

There are also seats outside that have views of the ocean. The Ocean Fitness Center has a 25-meter indoor pool, an 18-meter hydro pool, a bathtub, a sauna, and a steam room that anyone can use for free. The gym is big and fully stocked, and there are exercise classes every day, some of which are free for guests.

There is free parking, and the hotel is on the coast road in Salthill, across from the pier and Galway Bay. There is a 10-minute walk to Galway Golf Club and a 5-minute walk to Pearse Stadium.

The Huntsman Inn

A small hotel. Comfortable rooms. A great deal. The Huntsman Inn is only a 5-minute drive from Galway's busy city center. It has free Wi-Fi and private parking. The bar and restaurant at this small hotel are very popular, and they have a view of Lough Atalia. The award-winning restaurant uses the best local ingredients to make meals that are in season.

The modern rooms have a hairdryer, ironing board, and a TV with a DVD player. They also have a way to make tea and coffee. There are large, heated shower rooms with free toiletries in each room. The Huntsman offers a large breakfast menu in the morning, which includes a full Irish breakfast. You can get drinks at the bar, which has a lot of different kinds of wine and beer.

Live music is played at the Huntsman Inn every Saturday night, and there is a game night every Monday. Galway has beautiful beaches and a long walkway that makes it a popular place to go to the beach. The lively city center has many shops and is home to the Galway Atlantaquaria and the Galway City Museum. It only takes 10 minutes to drive to either one from the hotel.

The House Hotel

Cool. Great food. Great place to be. Women really like it. The House is a beautiful 4-star hotel in Galway's famous Latin Quarter. It is close to Quay Square and the Spanish Arch. The House Hotel is in an old stone house but has modern amenities and Art Deco decor inside.

Each room is decorated differently and has soundproof windows, a flat-screen satellite TV, and a safe for your PC. Simple and stylish. The House is right in the middle of Galway, just a 10-minute walk from both Galway Cathedral and the National University of Ireland. There are a lot of small, independent shops close by, and Salthill and its promenade are only a 15-minute walk away.

The Ardilaun Hotel

A calm environment. Quite romantic. This high-end 4-star hotel is perfectly situated on large private grounds, in the green suburb of Taylors Hill, just 1 km from Galway city center. It says that people can use the gym and park for free.

The Ardilaun is a famous place for business travelers and vacationers looking for high-end lodging in Galway City. It is close to gardens, beaches, shopping, theaters, and movies, as well as many outdoor activities.

The Ardilaun Hotel has a great leisure club with an 18-meter pool, hot bath, sauna, steam room, and high-tech gym. It is a peaceful place to stay.

Best Boutique Hotels

The Stop

There is a bed and breakfast. Very cute. Very cool. Great food. The coast is a half mile away and the city center is only 5 minutes away on foot. This building from the 1930s has stylish rooms and a modern feel all over, with modern art adding to the effect. It takes 15 minutes to walk to Eyre Square, which has many shops and restaurants.

Each room is designed differently and has its own bathroom and heating. You can also use the free WiFi. A cozy shared lounge with chairs is a great place to unwind. Every day, breakfast is served with food that comes from nearby farms. Salthill and the ocean are both easy to get to on foot. It's less than 1.5 km from Galway Railway Station.

Sea Breeze Lodge B&B Galway

There is a bed and breakfast. Beautiful land. Not like any other. Comfortable rooms. This 5-star bed and breakfast has a view of the beautiful Galway Bay. It also has free Wi-Fi, free parking, delicious breakfasts, and cozy rooms with plush memory foam pillows.

The Sea Breeze Lodge B&B Galway is only 3.5 km from the harbor and city center of Galway. The house is on Salthill's main coast road. Salthill is a seaside suburb of Galway. The cute and cozy en suite rooms all have wooden floors, central heating, hair dryers, tea/coffee makers, and flat-screen digital TVs. The rooms either have a view of Galway Bay or the well-kept grounds of the lodge. There are rooms with both queen-size and super-king-size beds.

Every room has a bed with a memory foam cushion. Each part of your body touches the surface of the memory foam mattress and gets the same amount of support because it molds to your shape. There is a tasty full Irish breakfast included in the price.

High-speed wireless broadband internet access is offered all over the Sea Breeze Lodge, which has a Wi-Fi hotspot. Sea Breeze Lodge is a great place to stay if you want to explore this beautiful part of Ireland. It has great views, is in a great spot, and has cozy rooms.

Glenlo Abbey Hotel

Beautiful place. Historic building. Beautiful views. A favorite among lovers. The 5-star Glenlo Abbey Hotel & Estate is only 2 miles from the center of Galway. It has free parking, a golf course, and views of Lough Corrib and the dramatic West of Ireland scenery.

The 138-acre golf course is next to a lake and has a 21-bay driving range and golf classes. At the Glenlo Abbey Hotel & Estate, the Pullman Restaurant on the Orient Express is a one-of-a-kind place to eat, and they serve afternoon tea every day. These antique Pullman train cars have been turned into restaurants while keeping their original look.

They have two dining rooms. You can also do falconry, shooting, and fishing on-site. Residents of the hotel can use the estate bicycles for free to go for a ride around Glenlo Abbey Estate. The Glenlo Abbey Hotel & Estate rooms all have a flat-screen TV, a marble bathroom with a power shower, free Wi-Fi, high-end toiletries, towels and slippers, and a marble bathroom. Palmers Bar & Kitchen is in the main hotel and is a great place for casual eating. It has a wide range of food options, a lively atmosphere, and cozy rooms. The River Room Restaurant has a beautiful setting.

The Nest Boutique Hostel

A hostel, Very cute, A great deal. Women really like it. The Nest Boutique Hostel is a place to stay in Galway. There are chairs in some rooms where you can relax. The Nest Boutique Hostel has free WiFi all over the building. Two kilometers away is Salthill, and three kilometers away is St. The front desk is open 24 hours a day, and there is a fireplace in the common room. There is limited free parking (5 spots, one of which is accessible) and it is first-come, first-served. It takes 1.7 km to get to Nicholas Collegiate Church. The house is 64 km from Shannon Airport.

Black Cat

Guest house or inn. A great deal. Women really like it. The Black Cat is in Galway, just 400 meters from Ladies Beach. It has a kitchen, rooms that don't smoke and free WiFi. Grattan Beach is only 700 meters away, St. Nicholas Collegiate Church is 2.4 km away, and Eyre Square is 2.7 km away. The Dublin Greyhound Stadium is 4 km away, and Ballymagibbon Cairn is 40 km away. Each room at the inn has a flat-screen TV.

All the rooms at Black Cat have their own bathroom with free items and a hairdryer. A stay at this hotel is 2.8 km from Galway Railway Station and 3 km from the National University of Galway. Shannon Airport is 83 km away and is the closest airport to Black Cat.

The Dean Galway

Hip. Full of life. Nice, soft beds. It opened in January 2022. There are free bikes, an outdoor pool, an exercise center, and a terrace at The Dean Galway in Galway. This 4-star hotel has free WiFi, room service, and a front desk that's open 24 hours a day.

There is a diner at the hotel that serves both American and Italian food. At the bar, people can get something to drink. Each room has a desk, a flat-screen TV with satellite stations, a minibar, a kettle, a shower, and free toiletries. Each room has its own bathroom, hairdryer, and bed linens.

You can also ask for vegetarian, dairy-free, or gluten-free choices. Eyre Square, Galway Railway Station, and Galway Greyhound Stadium are all popular places to visit near Dean Galway. Shannon Airport is the closest airport, which is 80 km away.

The Residence Hotel

Great place to be. Comfortable rooms. The Residence Hotel is in the nightlife district of Galway and has free WiFi. There are 20 differently designed rooms in the hotel. Each one has a flat-screen TV with Netflix and a coffee or tea maker. Galway's Latin Quarter has streets that look like they were built in the Middle Ages and lots of shops, cafes, bars, and restaurants. The Residence Hotel is right next to the 1520 Bar, which serves a daily fresh menu. You can also enjoy live music. There is a 5-minute walk between Eyre Square and Galway Station.

The G Hotel

Galway's g Hotel has undergone a €1 million renovation to become the most stylish hotel in western Ireland. The five-star resort, known for its natural light, high ceilings, and stunning views of Lough Atalia, has been updated with unique ground-floor rooms. The €1 million renovation aimed to maintain the hotel's signature rooms' stylish and classy vibe while incorporating a subtle sophistication. The new GEO restaurant and cocktail bar have been redesigned to feel more open and spacious, with a new garden patio and botanical theme. The GEO restaurant features statement chandeliers, smoked mirrors, and coral accents. The two Signature Lounges have been renovated to feel glamorous and high-class, with the Pink Room featuring blush pink velvets, tasseled chairs, and brass details, and the Blue Room with a ginger, charcoal, and rich wood color scheme.

Best Budget-Friendly Hotels
Nox Hotel Galway

In Galway, the Nox Hotel Galway is in a great spot—it's only a short walk to the city center. The Galway City Museum, Terryland Forest Park, and the NUIG Organic Garden are just a few of the popular places you can visit because of this. Deadmans Beach and a few other beaches are close by if you want to have fun at the beach.

Visit the sights for the day, then come back to this hotel for a well-deserved rest. The hotel has a bar where you can get a drink and talk to other guests. You could also go to your room right away and watch a bunch of movies in bed.

Clayton Hotel Galway

The Clayton Hotel Galway is a 4-star hotel in Galway. It has modern rooms and suites with air conditioning, beds with King Koil pillows, and big flat-screen TVs. You can get a free cereal breakfast, a full English or Irish breakfast, a vegetarian or vegan breakfast, or a gluten-free breakfast as a guest. You are also welcome to use the pool and fitness area, among other things.

For more fun, the hotel is close to a few places to visit. That's only a short drive away, so if you want to enjoy the ocean, go there. Eyre Square, Spanish Arch, Lynch's Castle, and Terryland Forest Park are some other interesting places to visit.

Flannery's Hotel

There is old-world charm and modern comfort at
Flannery's for all of its guests. It only takes five minutes
to drive to downtown, and it only takes ten minutes to get
to the airport. There are two restaurants on-site, and you
can also get room service. The Galwegian Restaurant
serves breakfast and dinner with food from around the
world. At Frankie's Bar and Bistro, you can watch all of
your favorite sports games. On the weekends, there is also
live folk music.

Fox B&B

It takes about 10 minutes to get to the Fox B&B from the
center of Galway. You can feel like you're in the country
while still being close to all the city's sights. You can
enjoy the hot, free breakfast and the free Wi-Fi that's
available all over the hotel. A real Irish bar is only a short
four-minute walk away and serves beer and food. Garden
views can be seen from most of the rooms. Couples can
enjoy a lovely stay at this bed and breakfast.

Clybaun Hotel

The Clybaun is in the middle, halfway between Galway and Salthill Resort. Many nice features are available at the fancy hotel, like a heated pool, exercise center, outdoor hot tub, and spa. All day, O'Gorman's Bar & Bistro serves lunch and bar food. From breakfast to dinner, you can eat hot food at the Maritime Restaurant. The Clybaun has planned events that the whole family can enjoy. You could also just chill out on the grounds and forget about your problems for a while.

The Ardilaun Hotel

The Ardilaun Hotel is the place to go if you want to find peace and quiet. It's in a Galway neighborhood, but it's still close enough to the city center that you can walk there. There is a sports club on site with a pool, sauna, steam room, and gym. The Avalon Health & Beauty Salon is a great place to get massages and beauty services. You can choose from a variety of eating options, from a breakfast buffet to a fancy dinner.

Anno Santo Hotel

The Anno Santo Hotel is in Galway's Salthill Resort and has been owned and run by the same family for three generations. With just 14 rooms. During your stay, you will get individual service. The beach is only a short walk away, and the center of Galway is only a short drive away. There is free Wi-Fi in all rooms, and the furniture is very nice. You can also grab a cup of tea at the cafe.

The White House

There are lovely views of either the Atlantic Ocean or the Burren Mountains from the rooms in the White House. Galway Golf Club and Salthill Beach are both only a short walk away. You can relax in your nice room, which has a couch and a tray for guests to use. There is also free Wi-Fi, a hot Irish breakfast, and parking on-site. It's only 1.5 miles (2 km) to the city center, where you can find shops and bars.

Amber Heights Guesthouse

The city center is only a short drive away, about 1.9 miles (3 km) from the Amber Heights Guesthouse. Each room has its own bathroom, free Wi-Fi, and cable TV. In the lounge room, you can use a computer and printer, and coffee and tea are served all day.

The aquarium and O'Connor's Pub are just across the street, and there is bus service to and from the city center.

Bunk Boutique Hostel

The Bunk Boutique Hostel is right in the middle of the city. There are rooms for both men and women, and some of them have separate bathrooms. There is free Wi-Fi, bag storage, and lockers available. Guests are welcome to use the kitchen and there are also snack machines for their convenience. There is a computer workstation with a printer in the guest room. It's easy to get to many famous spots, like Eyre Square and the Spanish Arch, thanks to its good location.

The Burren

CHAPTER FIVE

Famous Local Dishes and Drinks to Try in GALWAY

These hearty and filling meals give you a real taste of Ireland because they are made with local ingredients and traditional cooking methods.

Ireland's food scene is booming, and chefs all over the country are making delicious new dishes. But the old favorites will always be the best. These are the most authentic Irish recipes you should try. They use fresh seafood from Ireland's shores, beef and lamb raised on the country's green pastures, and a lot of different kinds of food grown in the country.

1. Irish Stew

Irish stew is the most popular dish in Galway, and it's now a standard dish in Ireland, eaten by people from all walks of life. Simple foods like potatoes, carrots, and onions are used, and they are cooked slowly with hard meat from a goat or any other animal.

This traditional stew has been around for hundreds of years. It was great for cooking tough foods like old mutton or lamb, especially in Galway's cold winters. People said to add pearl barley, a spoonful of roux, or chopped potatoes and let the stew simmer for a long time to keep it from being too watery. This kind of long cooking brings out the best in every taste.

These days, it's easy to find tender lamb in stores. It's cooked with stock and herbs like thyme, parsley, and bay leaves to give the taste more depth.

2. Boxty

Most Irish people say that the name of this dish comes from the Irish term arán bocht tí, which means "poorhouse bread." However, the dish is not bread at all; it's a cake that has been mashed with potatoes. Irish people eat potatoes all the time, so you'll find them in a lot of Galway food. For this meal, chop up raw potatoes and mix them with mashed potatoes. Along with the mashed potatoes, a mix of flour and salt is boiled. The potatoes are then cut up and fried in butter for more time. 'Boxty on the pan' means cooking the pancake with all of the Boxty inside, like a stuffed paratha. 'Boxty in the oven' means cooking the Boxty separately, then cutting it up and frying it. Boxty is eaten with smoked salmon and crème fraiche or bacon and eggs.

3. Colcannon And Champ

Mashed potatoes, cabbage, kale, butter, and cream are all mixed in this standard comfort food. Irish food from Galway that is served as a side dish with boiled ham or bacon mixed in. People usually add spring onions to it to make it taste better. It has a lovely Halloween link because surprises like a ring and a thimble are hidden inside it for kids and adults to find. Champ, on the other hand, is more like a soup. It has mashed potatoes and onions that have been chopped and cooked in butter or milk. Some people also like to add salt and pepper to the dish to make it taste better.

4. Coddle

Some people think that the word "coddle" comes from the way that items in a one-pot stew are slowly cooked, or "coddled." This is another tasty Galway, Ireland, meal that is cooked slowly and is often eaten as a leftover dish in Galway homes. In general, the Coddle is made up of sausages, bacon, onions, and potatoes that were left over from other meals. It can also be made with fresh sausages. Like stew, it is made by slowly cooking the ingredients in stock and steaming them in a pot for a long time. It is then served hot with fresh thyme on top. If you're in Dublin, near the River Liffey, The Woollen Mills is the best place to get a curl.

5. Cockles And Mussels

Because Ireland has some of the best seafood in the world, the Western area of Galway has some very tasty foods, like cockles, which are small saltwater clams, and mussels. There is a story about a beautiful young woman selling the fresh catch of the day on the streets of Dublin, and this food became more well-known when it was included in the song. You have to try these fish dishes when you go to Ireland. They are the best in Galway. Most of the time, cockles are cooked and served with crunchy chips.

6. Galway Oysters

Fresh mussels are another type of seafood that you should try in Galway. West of Ireland is known for having the best oysters in the country. The best oysters are picked in Clarinbridge, County Galway. You can also get it at Mourne Seafood Bar in Belfast, where it comes with a pint of Guinness. There are many Galway International Oyster and Seafood Festivals. At these, you can watch the Irish and World Oyster Opening or "shucking" Championships and eat other tasty Galway foods from over a thousand stalls.

7. Smoked Salmon

Irish people love smoked salmon made in the usual way even more than mutton stew. A lot of places offer microwaved salmon as smoked salmon, so don't go to a cheap restaurant and try them. You can trust the oak-smoked salmon from the Burren Smokehouse, the beechwood-smoked salmon from the Connemara Smokehouse, and the unique turf-smoked salmon from The Haven Smokehouse. These are all real Galway seafood restaurants that serve the freshest, tastiest fish.

8. Black And White Pudding

All over the world, black pudding is made by shaping a sausage made of pork meat, fat, and blood mixed with barley, suet, and oats. White pudding, on the other hand, has all the same fixings except for the blood. Today, people in Galway like to eat both of these puddings for breakfast, either with sautéed scallops, in croquettes, under-boiled eggs, or with salads and risottos. You can also add these as a garnish to ready-made soups, which will fill you up for a single meal.

9. Soda Bread

These are some of the foods that Irish people in Galway eat as a way to remember their families and old times. Since every family has their own soda bread recipe. This is some of Galway's best food, and the old recipes are still used in different parts of the city. You can call sosa bread a "quick bread," which means it's not made with yeast. Instead, baking soda is used to raise the bread. Some people like to put honey, sugar, or dried fruits on top of the sweet bread. Some people like to add nuts, bran, and oats to their food to make it healthier. While the basic ingredients of flour, baking soda, and buttermilk (which acts as a raiser) stay the same. There are both white and brown types of this traditional food in Galway for people to choose from.

10. Barmbrack

In Galway, this is another type of quick bread that is often filled with nuts and fruits and served with a cup of tea in the afternoon. In Galway, this tasty piece of bread is made with raisins, candied peel that has been steeped overnight in black tea and whiskey, and mixed spice. Irish grocery stores and bakeries still sell Halloween barmbracks that have a toy ring hidden inside. This is a practice that goes back a long time and is a popular food in Galway.

Best Places to Eat in GALWAY

Galway has been known for a long time as the food capital of the West of Ireland. Because the city is divided into different cultural areas, it has a wide range of high-end restaurants, from artisanal pie shops and wood-fired pizzerias to some of the best seafood places in the country. Below are list of our favorite places in Galway.

Aniar Restaurant

As of September 2012, Aniar was given the prestigious Michelin star, making it Galway's only restaurant with this honor. Aniar is a new and different kind of restaurant in Galway City that serves food based on its location on Dominick Street. When people talk about wine, they usually mean terroir, which is the mix of land, climate, and environment that gives each wine its unique flavor.

A restaurant called Aniar, which is run by the same people who own the restaurant next door, Cava, focuses on using natural, earthy ingredients from the area. "Salt beef, radish, kohlrabi, and hazelnut" could be a beginning. "Wild brill, celeriac, celery, clams, and lovage" could be a main course. For dessert, "seabuckthorn pannacotta, caramel, apple, and crumble" could be a treat. location: 53 Lower Dominick Street, Galway City, Ireland

Kai Café and Restaurant

Kai Café and Restaurant have a very simple philosophy: they only use fresh, organic food from local sources to make daily menus that are full of flavor, texture, and color. You might even get a flower that you can eat on your plate if you're lucky.

Each day's menus are different based on what's fresh and in stock from nearby sources. Head Chef Jess Murphy makes food with an artisanal touch by mixing her classical training in cooking with a love of unique, fresh seasonal food. She gets the best raw materials straight from the growers and watches over the whole cooking and preparation process until the food is ready to be served.

Chef Jess Murphy is from New Zealand but has lived in Ireland for a long time. Murphy first worked for Kevin Thornton in his Michelin-starred restaurant. After that, she went to Ard Bia and, finally, Bar 8, where she was named Best Chef in Connacht. The food is delicious and always based on what is in season and available nearby. location: Galway City, Ireland, on Sea Road

Ard Bia

When Food & Wine magazine named Ard Bia Nimmo's the Best Regional Restaurant a few years ago, the restaurant grew and grew. In the ancient Spanish Arch, there is an eclectic, arty dining room with a view of the Corrib. This room is famous for its delicious food made with the best local and seasonal ingredients. We like the mezze plate, the rib-eye steak with roasted shallot potato cake and Crozier Blue sauce, and the chickpea pancake with spinach and cheese. Upstairs at Ard Bia, there is a local studio with beautiful art that you can look at and talk about over a cup of coffee. Location: Long Walk, Spanish Arch, Galway City, Ireland

Oscars Seafood Bistro

The restaurant Oscar's Seafood Bistro has won many awards and is located on Dominick Street in the heart of Galway's West End. They have the best and freshest seafood, meats, and vegan meals in the area. Chef and co-owner Michael O'Meara runs the business with his team. You can get treats like their tasty Galway Hooker ale-battered fish and patatas bravas with remoulade sauce, their slow-cooked beef bourguignon with delectable buttery mash, or their hake that is impossible to chunk and served with sweet potato hash and fresh avocado salsa. Michael knows more about seafood than anyone else.

He wrote "SEA Gastronomy," which is the most complete book ever written about Irish seafood. A lot of people know Oscar's Seafood Bistro for its great seafood dishes and helpful service. Location: Dominick Street, Galway, Ireland, H91DXH7

Il Vicolo Restaurant

Il Vicolo is a great Italian restaurant with a view of the River Corrib. It is in the old, famous Bridge Mills building in Galway City and has won awards for its food. The restaurant serves the best rustic Italian food with a strong southern flavor. They do this with a lot of heart, soul, and hard work. Check out their modern Italian menu, which has Cicchetti that changes with the seasons along with pasta, rice, fish, and meat.

Their wine list is all Italian, with more than 75 wines from regions as far apart as the Italian Alps, the tip of the boot of the Italian Peninsula, and the island of Sicily.

Il Vicolo loves everything Italian and only uses the best Irish food, food from the surrounding area, and food from the Italian peninsula. This restaurant, Il Vicolo, is one of a kind in Galway's West End. It lets you enjoy the best of Italy while you eat, while the River Corrib flows by outside the old flour mill. Location: The Bridge Mills, Dominick St Lower, Galway, H91 R1WF

Brasserie on the Corner

Brasserie on the Corner is a great restaurant in the middle of Galway City that serves seafood and steak. You won't know what to order because there are so many seafood starts and beef, lamb, and seafood mains all made in the area. The original and varied menu and long list of boutique wines make sure that everyone can find something they like. The lovely, stylish, and cozy decor and the helpful staff make for a great meal. Do not miss.

Location: Eglinton Street, Galway City, Ireland

Lignum Restaurant

The old way of cooking over an open flame is called "lignum," which comes from the Latin word for "wood." Lignum was created by Chef Danny Africano and his highly skilled team of chefs. They have created one of the most amazing and renowned restaurants in Ireland that serves authentic Irish food.

The creative menu at Lignum shows that the chef knows how to get the most taste and nutrition out of foods. The dishes are packed with textures and flavors that go well together.

Lignum is in the town of Bullaun, in the east of County Galway, 6 km northeast of Loughrea. It has a dining area made of wood and glass that faces an old stone stable and is filled with light.

The walls are a bold black color, and the tables are big and rustic, made from ash. The restaurant has always gotten great ratings. In 2020, the Irish Times gave it nine out of ten stars and said it was "innovative, accomplished, and delicious." Location: Slatefort House, Bullaun, Co. Galway, H62 H798

White Gables

Irish food is served in a renovated stone cottage at a village crossroads in Moycullen. The White Gables Restaurant only serves traditional Irish food, mostly seafood, like fresh lobster from their fish tank. The warm, cozy red color, flowery lamp shades, and dark wood furniture paint a picture of Ireland from a different time. All of the fish is fresh from the boat, and you can also get meat. Fillet steak and t-bone are classic Irish dishes that you can order. Location: Moycullen, Galway, Ireland

Powers Thatch Pub and Restaurant, Oughterard

If you're living near Oughterard or traveling around Galway, you have to go to Powers Restaurant. It has some of the best Irish food you can find. With its unique traditional house setting, stylish but simple decor, and delicious food, this restaurant is a great place to eat. Head Chef Cillian Hanrahan runs the kitchen, which was set up with the help of top Galway chef Jess Murphy of Kai Café and Restaurant.

This arrangement has laid the groundwork for a menu that is always of very good quality. There are many meals to choose from, such as the creamiest seafood chowders, wings, steaks, monkfish, burgers, curry, salads, and a lot more. People like Powers because it has great food, a cozy atmosphere, and helpful, friendly staff.

Location: Main Street, Oughterard, Co. Galway, Ireland

Morans Oyster Cottage, Kilcolgin

Many years ago, Moran's Oyster Cottage was one of the best places to eat in the west of Ireland. The restaurant is in a thatch hut that is 250 years old and looks out over a part of Galway Bay. Some people also call it Morans of the Weir. It's one of the best-known bars and seafood places in Cork County. Michael Moran runs this family business. He is the seventh generation of the Moran family to run the restaurant. The restaurant serves only the freshest, best seafood. Some of the menu's mainstays are the delicious smoked salmon, oysters, lobster, and the newest catch from Galway Bay.

People come from all over the world to this seafood restaurant, which is full of character. Over the years, many people have made it their favorite place to eat, as you can see from the pictures on the walls. Now with a big deck with a view of the sea that is open all year and protected from the weather.

Location: Morans Oyster Cottage, The Weir, Kilcolgin, Co. Galway, Ireland

West Restaurant @ The Twelve

The West Restaurant in Barna is an up-to-date urban club-style restaurant on the second floor of The Twelve Hotel. The Twelve has a history of serving great food, and the West restaurant takes that to a whole new level. Stylish, classy, and sophisticated, it has American-style seats that give off an air of sophistication, making it the perfect place to indulge your taste buds. The menu has creative dishes that show off the best of Galway and the season's freshest products. This is a place for real foodies. This restaurant has won many awards and is only a 10-minute drive from Galway City Center. It is in the beautiful coastal town of Barna. Address: Barna, Co. Galway, Ireland

Guys Bar, Clifden

If you've been visiting Connemara all day, the only place you'll want to go is a cozy pub to cool off and think about what you saw. Guys Bar & Restaurant in Clifden is the right spot for you. This is one of Clifden's oldest bars. Its warm, country decor includes old traditional snugs and cozy corners with a roaring turf fire, making it a great place to hang out with family or friends. There are delicious meals on the menu for people of all ages and tastes, including fresh seafood, traditional stews, gourmet pizzas, rice dishes, and good veggie options. For babies, there is even a free bowl. A great place to eat in a relaxing setting when you're in Connemara.

Best Restaurants in GALWAY

The food in Galway is delicious, and the fish is especially good. It includes everything from small Galway cafés to places with Michelin stars. Galway food can be anything, from traditional Irish meals to new dishes cooked in the Irish style.

We all know that food is a big part of making a trip, but there's more to it than that. Check out these restaurants for some of the best food I've had in Galway. Come on!

1. Aniar

Aniar and Dela are both on the same street. People who love food will love this street, and if you're lucky, you'll spend most of your meals there. My favorite recipe is The Irish recipe, which was written by JP McMahon, who owns and runs Aniar and is also its head chef. He and his staff know everything there is to know about old and new Irish food. The people who run Aniar do it to honor Western Irish food.

It's not anything out of the ordinary during the day if you care about style. But when the candles are lit, it turns into a beautiful and cozy place. But you're here for the food that has earned them a Michelin star, and they've kept that standard up since 2013.

You could try trout with sheep's yogurt, sea buckthorn, beef nasturtium, and pumpkin miso on an example 18-dish tasting plate. They aren't giving away much, but the point is for you to trust them. Save a spot and enjoy what I think is one of the best places in Galway.

location: Dominick Street, Galway City

2. Eán

Éan began by only delivering food. It's interesting that the people who own Éan also own Loam, a restaurant with a Michelin star (see above). So, you should enjoy what this café has to offer, though it won't cost as much as the Loam.

I stopped by not long ago for a quick snack and coffee. It was the smell of the kitchen that drew me in. Éan feels like a folky, peaceful, and thought-out place to be inside. It's just right for two people because it's not very big.

At Éan, you'll eat well. You can pick from a wide range of tasty, sweet, and spicy croissants. There is a place with Connemara shrimp, preserved lemon, and dino kale for lunch. You should also try one of their bread sandwiches, like the one with za'atar, summer squash, organic leaves, and organic beets.

In the evening, you'll be served bigger meals, like a €40 lamb shoulder with dumplings, black garlic, and shiitake mushrooms that serve two, as well as squid toast with blonde miso and bonito, and so on. It's great to see tastes that are so different from those in Dublin. Visit Éan!

Location: Druid Lane, Galway City

3. Pullman Restaurant

Okay, this is a unique event. The restaurant at the Pullman is housed in two original Orient Express coaches that have been beautifully brought back to their former glory. You can find them on the grounds of the five-star Glenlo Abbey hotel, farm, and golf course, which is always booked up. You should spend at least one night at the Glenlo Abbey Hotel if you can. Book a table at The Pullman restaurant, and then while you're there, enjoy the rest of the beautiful land.

Drinks are a great way to start your Pullman meal. Their whiskey sours, Pullman "Train Smash", Irish Mules, or even "The Grumpy Conductor" might tempt you. You can get the pearl barley risotto, the velvet pork with apple, carrot, and pickled mustard seed, or the scallops with wood sorrel and pancetta for dinner. After that, serve Bailey's ice cream, Cuinneog buttermilk cream, and tiramisu. "Pullman's" gets a strong "yes" from me. You should go there. Location: Glenlo Abbey Hotel and Estate

4. Kai

The Kai restaurant is a cool place that's only 8 minutes' walk from the center of Galway. I love how this place makes me feel. It has stone walls, split-level ceilings (the open kitchen has a glass area that's higher than the rest), and a lot of different types of finishes.

A shout-out to their retro wooden seats, like the church pews and the chairs that look like they came from an Irish public school in the 1960s. If you have kids, this is also a great place for the whole family.

You can expect updated takes on old favorites when you go to Kai for lunch. Feel free to try the chickpea filo pies, the fancy fish fingers, and the spicy black bean nachos. For dinner, choose the Roscommon lamb chops with beetroot picada and green tahini or the Rossaveal hake with burnt butter cauliflower and romesco.

Don't skip the dessert. Their strawberry and malt ice cream, Hokkaido pumpkin pie, dark chocolate and, almond pudding with burnt butter ice cream all look great. Kai is an everyday place that is nice and doesn't charge too much for good food. Location: Sea Road, Galway's West End

5. The Dough Bros Pizza

When we go back to Galway City, we find the famous Dough Bros pizza place. These guys have been in business for almost ten years, which is pretty long for an Irish small business. They are a Galway institution for wood-fired pizza, and they are also cheap and great for quick, relaxing meals.

There are many types of pizza to choose from, such as the "posh pepperoni" pizza with Toons Bridge fior di latte, the ham and mushroom pizza, or the kale-based pizza. They also have vegan pizza, garlic bread, and garlic dip which are all vegan.

I forgot to say that garlic dip in Ireland is surprisingly good. I would try to get a garlic dip from a place like this. Go to The Dough Bros. if you want to eat somewhere relaxed and simple with a younger crowd. Location: Middle Street, Galway

6. Owenmore Restaurant

The Owenmore restaurant is in the Ballynahinch Castle, which has four stars (it should have five stars). There are several two-seater tables by the floor-to-ceiling windows that run along the dining room's walls. These windows let you see the beautiful scenery of Lough Inagh and the surrounding area of Connemara.

The manor house was recently redecorated to match its period, so the decor is elegant and traditional as a whole. I think you should stay at Ballynahinch Castle for one or two nights. So, you can eat as much as you want at Owenmore restaurant, which has food that is miles better than any other 4-star hotel's food.

You can start with the Cleggan crab, the whipped Galway goat's cheese, or the pork scrumpet with smoked black pudding. After this, have a black sole on the bone with orange and cardamom beurre blanc or a piece of beef in Bourguignon sauce.

The dessert menu is also inspired by French food with a touch of Irish food. A burnt lemon cremeux with meringue and raspberry sorbet is one of these. Another is a dark chocolate delice with peated whiskey ice cream. What a spread, huh? Location: Recess, Connemara

7. Loam

Loam got a Michelin star in 2015 and has kept it ever since. It feels like an art gallery and is well-known in the foodie world. The whole thing is an experimental show. There are both public dining tables with plants on them and private round tables for pairs or smaller groups. The inside looks like a mix of "Japandi minimalism (Japanese and Scandinavian) meets mid-century industrialist."

As you'd expect from a high-end silver service restaurant, their food is really good but comes in small portions. You can get meat boards with Gubbeen salami and air-dried lamb from Connemara, or you can get cheese boards with different kinds of oozy cow's milk cheese. You'll be surprised because the food changes every day based on what's in season.

Another dish on the sample menu is smoked eel with tomato and cucumber. There is also lamb, turnip, broad bean, squid, shiitake mushrooms, and egg. In Loam, the execution is very simple, but the cooking skill behind the scenes is very good. In Galway, this dinner is well worth the money. Location: Fairgreen Road, Galway City

8. The Quay Street Kitchen

The Quay Street Kitchen (QSK) is in Galway's cultural area, also known as The Latin area. This makes it a bit of a tourist spot. That being said, "touristy" doesn't always mean bad, unless it's meant to be a tourist trap. By chance, QSK is in the middle, and it's become popular because, well, it's popular!

It's a great place to grab a quick lunch if you're new to the city while you wait to check in or out of your hotel. There are seats outside where you can watch people. If you'd rather stay inside, the pub has a classy look and live music.

The dinner is all about vegan and gluten-free food. There are a lot of quinoa salads, Irish seaweed bread with almond feta, fish and chips, lamb shank, Shepherd's Pie, chicken and quinoa stew, and veggie sandwiches to choose from. You can learn a lot about Galway and its food at this restaurant. Location: The Latin Quarter, Galway city

9. Ard Bia At Nimmos

The Ard Bia at Nimmo's is right next to the Spanish arch from the Middle Ages, which runs along The Port of Galway. We stayed close during a storm, and Nimmo's small but stoney outside held up well against the wind and rain! Regardless of the weather, this is the best place to be if you want to be near the water.

The inside is "rustic-Irish-folk," which means there are waxy candle arbors, water carafes, dried flower pots, water rings on old wooden tables, and deep window sills. To put it another way, old Ireland meets new Ireland.

For breakfast, try chorizo and red pepper hash, hot cured mackerel with brown bread and garlic sauce, or granola with roasted rhubarb and pear. You'll eat Rueben melts, harissa lamb shoulder, and potato and herb rosti for lunch.

Dinner service gets angry Lots of different kinds of food are served, like hand-rolled tagliatelle with pumpkin and herb pesto, pumpkin pie with cinnamon mascarpone for dessert, and more. Location: Spanish Arch, Galway city

10. Morans Oyster Cottage

The cute thatched house with red windows and doors is Moran's. It is located on the weir of the Dunkellin and Clarenbridge Rivers. About a 35- to 40-minute drive from Galway City to the middle of nowhere, so this is going the extra mile... I'm sure you won't be sorry you put in the work, though.

As you might expect from an Irish bar, the inside has stone walls, a thatched roof, flower plates in display cabinets, shiplap ceilings, and a lot of pine furniture. I have no idea why the Irish are so crazy about pine. If you want to enjoy a Galway Hooker, make sure you get the pale ale and find a seat inside or on a bench by the water.

Since oysters grow so well along the coast, the Irish have been eating them for a very long time. Because of this, Moran's has a special menu just for oysters, which includes Clarenbridge and Gigas rock oysters.

Fish and chips, crab claws, prawn cocktails, seafood soup, and New Quay lobster are some of the things you can get from their main menu. This is a must-see for fish lovers who want to see more than just Galway City.

location: Kilcolgan, County Galway

11. Dela Restaurant

It's tucked away on Dominick Street, which is a foodie area that isn't as busy with tourists as Shop Street, which has all the gift shops, pubs, and chain restaurants. We went there for lunch, and the owner was very nice and gave us a seat by the window.

Get Dela's full Irish breakfast if you come in the morning. No matter how you cook your eggs—fried or scrambled—they will taste great! You can get a good cup of coffee in the morning there because mine was silky smooth. Another great thing about their breakfast is their buttermilk pancakes and eggs Benedict.

In the evening, you can eat wild venison with red Russian kale, harvest veggies, and mash, seabass fillet, or pork shoulder bonbons. You will also have a lot of vegetarian and gluten-free choices. In general, the atmosphere is very relaxing, calm, and warm. I think you should get a small window seat for two. Location: Dominick Street Lower, Galway City

Galway Twelve Tribes families (see p15.)

CHAPTER SIX

The Best Bars, Clubs & Nightlife in GALWAY

Galway's nightlife is one of the city's best parts. It's full of young people having fun, including college students, locals, seasonal workers, and of course, young visitors who come to have fun all the time.

There are late-night bars all over the city that are open until 2 a.m. and there are also great clubs where you can dance until the wee hours of the morning. Most of the clubs are in the city center, close to Eyre Square, where taxis, hotels, bars, and everything else you might need are easy to get to. There are also a lot of stag and hen parties, so the club scene is never dull.

Galway has some of the best bars in the West of Ireland. It has all the things you need for a great night out with friends. There are Traditional Bars, Gastropubs, Cocktail Bars, and Sports Bars in Galway. These places to drink are always big, and the beers never stop coming.

Carbon

On Eglinton Street, just off Eyre Square, Carbon is a famous place to dance. Now with live bands, new shows, and a lot more. Every day, food is served in the bar.
Area: Eglinton Street, Galway City, Ireland

Coyotes Late Bar and Club

This is Galway's first American-themed bar that was built just for that reason. It has a sports bar area, two dance floors, a bucking bronco (a mechanical bull) area, Karaoke, a pool table, a piano, dancers, and singers. All of their bars can be reserved for parties and other special events. All of the parties are set up and planned to fit.
Area: Forster Street, Galway City, Ireland

Electric Garden

Electric is Galway's most exciting place to go for more than one thing. Electric is a unique place for nightlife. It's been the site of music and art fairs, club nights, live shows, and food and drink events. These places are meant to make you feel good, think hard, and most importantly, dance.

Area: 36 Upper Abbeygate Street, Galway City, Ireland

Karma

When Karma Club Galway started in December 2002, it got a lot of good reviews. Karma Club Galway is one of the best places to go clubbing in Ireland. It's right in the middle of Galway in Eyre Square and has 4 floors full of fun things for young workers to do. Their VIP room, the Shadow Lounge, can be booked privately for any event. Open Wednesday through Sunday.

Area: William Street, Galway City, Ireland

Halo

Halo is the place to let loose and cause trouble. It's right in the middle of Galway, and every Friday and Saturday night they serve drinks and fun. Take off your mask, skip your bedtime, and put on your dancing shoes.

Halo is the best place in Galway for a night of fun with friends and family, whether it's a birthday party, a work social, or a hen party. This place only has one rule: leave your halo at the door!

Area: 36 Abbeygate Street Upper, Galway City, Ireland

Róisín Dubh

Róisín Dubh is without a question one of the best comedy and music venues in the country. It brings well-known artists to the city and gives up-and-coming artists a chance to perform. It's one of the best places to see the best national and foreign acts because it has a great vibe, great staff, and a real love for music and comedy. There has been a theater in Róisín Dubh for a long time. A lot of great bands, like Stewart Lee, Phill Jupitus, and Rich Hall, say it's one of their top ten favorite places to play in the world.

Roisin Dubh is also the person who makes the Galway Comedy Festival happen.

Strange Brew has been on Thursday nights for more than 12 years. It's been going for a long time and is one of Ireland's longest-running club nights. It's been very important in giving alternative acts a chance to play in a town where most venues prefer a more straightforward approach to live music. There are a lot of popular alternative bands in Ireland right now, like Two Door Cinema Club, Villagers, Le Galaxie, Delorentos, Jape, and And So I Watch You From Afar. They all started by playing free shows at Strange Brew the first few Thursday nights.

This isn't all that Róisín Dubh does. He also promotes the Galway International Arts Festival Big Top and brings a huge range of bands to Seapoint, the Town Hall Theatre, and the Black Box.

Area: 9 Dominick Street Upper, Galway Ireland

The Pins GastroBar

The cozy atmosphere of The Pins Gastropub makes it the heart and soul of The Twelve Hotel in Barna, which has won many awards.

The Pins Gastropub gives guests a real taste of the West of Ireland and is a favorite among both locals and tourists. The food menu has a mix of plates and bar bites that are inspired by the seasons. At the bar, their famous mixologists and sommeliers serve craft beers, rare drinks, and old wines. They also have a heated, shaded terrace called Nóin where you can eat outside.

Pizza Dozzina at The Pins Gastropub serves traditional Italian pizzas as well as locally inspired dishes like "The Prom Walk," "The Spanish Arch," and "The Barna Crossroads." You can watch your pizza being made in the beautiful MV Napoliforni stone oven. Pizza Dozzina is the place to go if you want to find genuine local ingredients and an authentic pizza oven along with the best pizza. They also make gluten-free versions of all of their tasty pies.

Area: Barna Rd, Freeport, Barna, Co. Galway, H91 Y3KA

Busker Brownes Gastropub

The bar and restaurant are great places to hold
One place, three bars, and 400 years of experience... People can do many things at Busker's. It has great food and a wide range of live music in a relaxed setting.

There is room to dance downstairs, and there are cozy seats and tables for groups. The Hall is on the third floor, up above. It is a beautiful room with stone walls, high ceilings, and leaded windows. For good reason, it's one of the best places to have a party in Galway! All three bars can take reservations. Just walk in or call 091 563377 and ask what they can do for you.

Busker Brownes will make sure you get all three meals a day. Breakfast starts at 10 a.m., lunch at noon and dinner at 5 p.m. If you want to eat out in Galway, go to Busker Brownes for your next meal. They serve tasty food all day.

"You can't have a night out in Galway without going to Busker Brownes." Area: Cross Street Upper, Galway

Galway Hooker

We are a small, independent brewery in the west of Ireland. Our goal is to make natural, full-flavored beers of the highest standard. When we use the best products and old-fashioned brewing methods together, we make all of our beers. As a result, the beer has won many awards, including being named Ireland's Best Beer twice.

We think that beer is like food: the more natural and fresh it is, the better. Because of this, our beers don't have any additives and are made with just sugar, hops, yeast, and water. We are excited about making new and interesting beers that are full of flavor and personality. People in Ireland think of Galway Hooker as a leader in the field of craft beer because it was the first constant pale ale made there. It has now become a strong favorite among beer lovers.

A first-cousin duo named Aidan Murphy and Ronan Brennan opened the brewery in 2006. Having worked in breweries all over the world for more than ten years, Aidan is an expert in the field. He also has a master's degree in beer and liquor making. He takes care of all of our guests and knows everything there is to know about craft beer. Area: Carrowkeel, Co. Galway Ireland

Carroll's on Dominick Street

Carroll's is one of the best places to hang out in the afternoon or get drinks before going out at night. It's in Galway's hip Westend. It is close to all of the best places to see live music and eat in the West End, making it a great spot for getting together with family and friends.

Going inside Carroll's is like going back in time and finding something delightfully old. The beer garden behind the bar, which was just fixed up, is a great place to have drinks before going out on the town.

And if you like sports, you'll enjoy the big screens around the pub and maybe a quick stop at the bar next door! On the weekends, they have live traditional music, and sometimes they play darts.

Area: 39 Lower Domnick Street Galway

Bierhaus

Huge selection of craft beer and grub
Bierhaus is Galway's first craft beer bar. It opened in 2005 in the middle of the city's West End and is now one of the most popular places for famous Galwegians to hang out.

Bierhaus has 24 taps that serve craft beers from around the world and Ireland. They also have a drink menu and serve seasonal wine. Jack Considine and Conor Lynam, who own the bar, are big fans of craft beer, modern music, and cocktails. If you want to know what to drink, you should talk to them.

The kitchen is open seven days a week and serves a range of hot dogs and standard grilled sandwiches.

Folks who live in Galway love Bierhaus for its laid-back vibe and fun weekend gigs. If you're planning a trip there, you should make time to visit.

Area: 2 Henry St, Galway Ireland

CHAPTER SEVEN

The Most Romantic Things to Do In GALWAY

Galway is a lovely city on Ireland's west coast. There are many romantic things for couples to do there. Here are five cool things to do in Galway with your sweetheart:

- ♥ Go for a stroll along Quay Street and the Latin Quarter. Walk slowly with a partner along Quay Street and the Latin Quarter. The narrow cobblestone streets are lined with brightly colored buildings, busy bars, restaurants, and small shops, making the area look beautiful and romantic.

- ♥ Claddagh Ring Experience: The Claddagh ring is an old Irish sign of friendship, love, and loyalty. Claddagh Gold by Thomas Dillon is the oldest jewelry store in Ireland. You can do the Claddagh Ring Experience there. With the help of a skilled jeweler, you and your partner can learn about the past of the ring and even make your rings.

♥ Salthill Promenade at Sunset: Go to Salthill Promenade, a beautiful beach spot just outside of the city center. As the sun goes down over Galway Bay, take a romantic walk along the shore. You'll be blown away by the view, which will stay with you forever.

♥ River tour on the Corrib: Take a leisurely trip down the River Corrib. This river runs through Galway and gives you beautiful views of the Spanish Arch and Galway Cathedral, among other sights. No matter what you'd like, you can choose a daytime or evening trip.

♥ Take a quiet lunch in Eyre Square. Fill a basket with tasty Irish treats and find a shady spot in the square. This central park is surrounded by lots of trees and plants, making it a great place for a quiet lunch with your partner. After your picnic, why not grab a drink at The Hardiman?

Galway City's most romantic spots

Galway Market is a lovely spot

Galway Market is a lovely place to take a walk and enjoy the atmosphere while looking at tasty treats for a picnic or giving handmade gifts to that special someone. This is especially true around Christmas and other big holidays. The Galway Market is a popular spot for couples looking for something to do during the day because it has music and a nice atmosphere.

Palas is a great place to go to the movies.

If you're sick of going to boring movie theaters that don't cater to special events, then stop going to those places and go to Palas Cinema instead. You can try tasty food and drinks, like cool cocktails, before or after the movie you've chosen. In addition, there is a nice outdoor area to enjoy, interesting art on display, and a generally friendly setting that makes watching movies a pleasure.

You should stay at the G Hotel & Spa.

If you want to spend your love weekend in a nice hotel, The g Hotel & Spa is a great choice. The Salthill Hotel is right next door to this spotless designer hotel. Both have rooms that exude luxury and spa services that you and your special someone can enjoy. This top location is without a doubt one of the best hotels Galway has to offer. It has a stylish bar serving tasty drinks and a wonderful thermal room that makes your stay even more relaxing.

The food at Sangria Tapas Restaurant is great.

You can also go to one of the city's great clubs or go for a walk in the countryside, but you should also think about trying some delicious Spanish food. You can get a real taste of Spain at Sangria Tapas Restaurant, which is in a beautiful spot that's great for a romantic evening. It's one of the best Spanish restaurants in the area, and they also serve veggie and vegan food. You and your loved one can have the romantic evening you deserve there.

Take a walk in Coole Park.

A walk in Coole Park is a great thing to do during the day or after a big meal to burn off some calories. You might even want to have lunch with your partner there. This park is a beautiful 1,000-acre nature reserve that is full of history. You can enjoy the lush scenery and maybe even grab a drink and a bite to eat at the park's restaurant.

The Best Date Ideas In Galway

TEA AND TALKS

A coffee date is a great way to spend the afternoon with someone, whether it's a first date or a get-together with someone you already know. A lot of cozy and unique cafés can be found in Galway, so there are lots of spots to meet new people over a tasty cup of coffee.

One of the best places to get coffee in Galway is Coffeewerk + Press in the Latin Quarter. Their cozy room upstairs is a great place to hang out with a friend over a cup of coffee. Serving gourmet coffee, and every cup tastes great!

Kali Coffee Bar is a cozy and friendly little coffee shop in Salthill. This is a great place to stop by after a romantic walk along the Prom because they serve tasty, smooth drinks. You can even share a coffee flight with your special someone, which is a great way to try a lot of different drinks.

Another great coffee shop with a great vibe is Urban Grind. They serve delicious lunch! City Grind is a stylish place in Galway's West End that's great for a first date or a hundredth. Their back patio with chairs under a roof is a beautiful place to fall in love.

DRINKS AND DINNER

In Galway, there are a lot of great bars and restaurants. It doesn't matter where you are in your love journey—there's a spot that will make you feel great on any given night.

To Have for Dinner...

If you want to spend an evening with candles in a hidden Venice, Il Vicolo is the place to go. This Italian place has a great atmosphere and a menu with tasty dinner and drink options. This is just the right amount of hot and relaxing.

In Galway's Westend, Deli La Tasca is a great place to get tasty snacks. This is a cozy and private place with lots of candles, Spanish wines, and tapas boards that you can share. This is a great place for you and your partner to feel love.

Seven Bar and Restaurant is a great place to go if you want a more relaxed but still friendly atmosphere. This is a great place to have dinner and drinks with someone you care about because the food is delicious and the drinks are great.

To Get Drinks...

People in Galway know and love the Skeff Bar! This is a great place to grab drinks with that special someone. It's in Eyre Square. This is a great place to spend an evening because it has a beautiful interior, great drinks, and live music.

People say that the Blue Note is the "beating heart of Galway's Bestend." So it makes sense that you come here to find out what your beating heart wants! Spending the night here with your partner will help you connect deeply and meaningfully, whether you're dancing or not. With its spinning dance ball and great music, The Blue Note is a great place to relax.

Bierhaus feels real and has a long list of handmade beers from around the world and in the United States. There are also some pretty tasty cocktails at the pub. For a date night, that sounds like a pretty good mix! There's nothing else you could want. Beirhaus is a modern standard with a laid-back vibe that's great for a romantic evening in Galway.

AN AFTERNOON AT THE MOVIE

Love, Lights, and Camera! A cozy movie date is sometimes all you need. Hold on tight to your partner and enjoy a movie on the big screen! The movies in Galway always have something good showing!

Pálás Cinema is a one-of-a-kind retro escape that shows some great movies. This is a great place for a date night because it shows special versions of old movies, new movies, and locally made films that were not made by a studio. You and your partner can also enjoy a great time at the bar upstairs. A night at Pálás is perfect and is sure to make two people fall in love.

The Eye Cinema in Wellpark has a huge collection of movies and showings. A great movie experience that is even better now that it's in a theater! Get close to your partner and maybe get a big bowl of popcorn for two. Even better, check out what The g Hotel and Eye Cinema are calling "The Ultimate Date Night" deal. After a wonderful meal at The g, go to Eye Cinema to see any movie you want!

Budget Things To Do in GALWAY

The best thing about Galway for tourists is that you can walk everywhere. As soon as you get there, take a stroll through the city. Pubs with lots of people, small shops, and winding cobblestone streets full of students, artists, writers, and crafters can be found there. You may even hear Gaelic. The island of Inis Mor is a good place to spend the day. The ocean air and beautiful scenery at Inis Mor will make you feel better when you get back. Also, no matter how cold it is on the island, don't forget to put on sunscreen.

WILD ATLANTIC WAY

We spent three days in Dublin and then went west. On the way, we stopped at the diner in Ballinasloe for a quick lunch. The Galway Food Tour and the bars and live music in the Latin Quarter were some of the things we did during our three nights in Galway. Moving on, spend a few nights in Doolin, Co. Clare, and visit The Buren, Inis Oirr, Aran Island, and the local pubs.

This was a four-day trip with lots of beautiful views through Kerry and around the lakes of Killarney on a rainy, foggy day. We liked everything, but the different scenery at each spot caught our attention. We all felt like this was just a taster for when we came back soon. To be fair, we went in August.

The roads are narrow, and during the busiest holiday times, there may be a problem with camping vans and big tour buses blocking some of the most popular sights. Cars have to move out of the way, and the hedgerows give them small scratches. Be careful, because there are ditches next to the roads that are hard to see because they are overgrown with plants and may look like solid ground.

ST. NICHOLAS' COLLEGIATE CHURCH

There are narrow, winding streets and a busy market all around Ireland's biggest medieval church.

This beautiful church is just around the corner from Tig Coili, down Market Street. It was built in 1320 and is dedicated to the patron saint of sailors. Christopher Columbus went there in 1477. Read all the handouts; they have a lot of useful information. If you happen to be there while a tour group is looking around, you can hear everything the guide has to say. After that, you should go across the street to Sheridan's Cheese Mongers.

GALWAY CATHEDRAL

We were on a tour with Gate 1 Travel, and Galway Cathedral was one of the things we had to see when we got there. The amazing Cathedral was made with rock from the area and marble from Connemara. With its flags, marble floors, stained glass windows, altars, cupola, and THAT big pipe organ, the church is truly beautiful. The sign with JFK on it stuck out in my mind. YOU HAVE TO SEE THIS CHAPEL! ONE OF THE BEST SIGHTS I'VE EVER SEEN!

HWY RIVESIDE

It was fun to walk along the river and see both new and old buildings, as well as interesting scenery and, of course, the river.

BEACHES IN SALTHILL

I had no idea I would get a tan in Ireland!! Clean, fun, and quiet beaches. Good for families. There are no lifeguards, so watch out. People from the US, know that the water is beautiful but very cold!

SALTHILL PROMENADE

If I lived close enough to this beautiful walkway that I could walk to it, I would be very thankful. On a nice day, it is very crowded with people walking with their dogs, kids, bikes, and roller skates. But it is a beautiful walk with lots of spots to stop, take a deep breath, and watch the world go by.

QUAY STREET

A must if you visit Galway...it's vibrant with street entertainers of the highest caliber. .musicians with great ability all in a pedestrian area with shops selling everything from funny Irish souvenirs to musical instruments ..good pubs with live music sessions and good food. The friendly Irish know how to enjoy themselves...

CONNEMARA NATIONAL PARK & VISITOR CENTRE

Connemara National Park is one of Ireland's six National Parks. The Visitor Centre for the National Park is situated beside Letterfrack Village. Entrance to the National Park grounds and walks (Diamond Hill), exhibition, and Audio Visual is free. The Visitor Centre is the starting point for the Diamond Hill walk.

Kylemore Abbey is a must-see and Diamond Hill is a great hike for all levels. There are long and short paths and it is accessible for people of any fitness level,

GALWAY BAY

The first trip wasn't in August, but in June 2020, so there weren't as many people on the streets, and I could take my time. I used to live in Seattle and now I live in Arizona. Being near the water again in this magical town on the Atlantic Ocean made me feel like everything I had lost was found again. You should think about going to Galway when you go to Ireland because you will fall in love with it like I did. Going back to Ireland in 2024 is on my list of things to do, and Galway is where I plan to stay.

Go to Merlin Woods.

Magic Woods is a great (and free) place to get away from the city without taking a full-day trip from Galway.

A huge area of urban forest surrounds the city. Some parts are bare limestone, which makes you feel like you're in a forest version of The Burren.

Go to Charlie Byrne's shop.

This cute little shop has over 100,000 books, making it a great place to spend a rainy day in Galway with kids. It's also one of the free things to do in Galway, though you'll want to buy a lot of things.

At Charlie Byrne's, you can find both new and used books. They even have books in foreign languages and a whole area of books for kids. There are many places here where you can learn about Galway and its past.

The bookshop has grown and changed several times since it first opened in 1989. In 2014, it was named the Best Bookshop in Ireland.

CHAPTER EIGHT
GALWAY Money Saving Tips

- If you want to save money while still getting full, eat bar food. There are pubs of all shapes and sizes in Galway, so take your time and look around until you find one with a good vibe and a great crowd.
- Don't drink as much; Ireland's bar culture can hurt your wallet. To keep costs down, drink at home, go to happy hours, or make one pint last all night. Galway is a town full of students, so there are lots of bars and happy hours where you can save money.
- Stay with a local. Couchsurfing lets you meet people in the city who are willing to host you for free and teach you about it. It's the best way to meet people in the area.
- Take a free walking tour. This is a great way to learn about the past of the city and get a feel for it. For cheap, it's the best way to get a feel for the place.
- Get dinner early. If you eat early (usually before 6 p.m.), many restaurants offer cheap dinner choices. For less money, you won't have as many options because it's a set menu.
- Bring a water bottle. You can drink tap water here, so bring a water bottle that you can use again and again to save money and the environment. Each LifeStraw

bottle has a built-in filter that makes sure the water inside is always clean and safe.

- You want to enjoy treats, a little more luxury than usual, and some time to relax on your holiday. You don't want to ruin that by trying to save money, but you also want your money to go as far as possible so that you can buy as many good things and great memories as you can.

No matter how much money you have, these below tips will help you save on things you need so you can spend that extra money on fun things. These tips are not at all meant to make your trip to Ireland mean or bad.

1. Take the hump route

When it's high season, like in Ireland in June, July, and August, as well as the weeks before and after St. Patrick's Day, everything about a trip costs more. This includes flights, hotels, and rental cars. You can save a lot of money by traveling in April, May, or September, which are the middle months.

Don't worry about the weather; no one goes to Ireland for the weather. It's almost certain that it will rain in August or July or almost certain that it will shine in September. In Ireland, everything is always a crap shoot.

It will also be less crowded at attractions, restaurants, and other places you visit, so there won't be as many lines and things will be usually calmer.

2. Think about other places to stay

You might want to do something different for at least part of your trip if you usually stay in a hotel.

Families and groups that want to stay in one place for three nights or more should check out Airbnb. There are some great places to stay in Dublin, Kerry, and Galway. If you're traveling with four or more people, you can save a lot on hotels without giving up any comfort. You'll save enough that you can eat breakfast at a nearby café if you don't want to make it yourself.

Also, think about B&Bs, even if you've never stayed in one before. But don't just look in the most obvious places; B&Bs in the middle of towns are usually more expensive and less personal. You can save money by staying just a few miles away. Some of the best and most interesting places to stay in Ireland are farms or country house B&Bs that aren't on the main tourist trail.

3. Stay put and loop the loop

This way of traveling can not only save you money but also make your trip more interesting and relaxed. Choose one or two places to stay for a few nights each instead of going to a new place every night. Then, each day, tour from your base in big loops. You'll feel more at home in your new place and get to know the people who live there better.

You can do this in any type of lodging. If you stay longer, you'll get better deals, which often include free dinners and/or the third night. Self-catering is also an option, which is a great choice that is very popular with Irish people for good reason. While hotels are more expensive, this is a great way to save money and stay in a place for a short time. It's also nice to have a home away from home.

You can stay in Kilkenny for four days and visit interesting places in Carlow, Wexford, Waterford, Laois, Kildare, and Tipperary. You can also take a day trip to Dublin.

You can stay in Ballingeary, Cork, for four days and do the Ring of Kerry, the Ring of Beara, Malin Head, a tour of West Cork, and a day trip to Cork City.

You've seen a lot in about a week, but you've only stayed in two places.

4. Book late... or early

A lot of websites are specialized in getting rid of last-minute hotel rooms that haven't been sold. If you want to play it safe, "last minute" can mean up to a few weeks in advance. If you're more into excitement, it can mean just a few hours.

We get new deals from Hotwire every few minutes, and you can also get great deals on hotels at the last minute by getting the Hotel Tonight app.

There are often deals of 60–70% off top hotels, which can save you a lot of money. There is some risk, and sometimes you'll only know the general area of the hotel and not its name, but you can be sure that something will come up and you will never be without a place to stay, even during the busiest times.

5. Get a smaller car to rent

This isn't just to save money; many of the most famous tourist spots are in remote areas with narrow roads, making it much easier to get around. But you can save a lot of money. Not only are smaller cars cheaper to rent, but they are also cheaper to drive. Since gas prices in Ireland are so high, this can save you a lot of money.

6. Get a card from Heritage

I'll say it again: GET A HERITAGE CARD! It's the best deal in Ireland. Get a copy. Make use of it. Tell everyone you know who is going to Ireland to do the same thing.

Many places, including some of the best places to visit in Ireland, will let you in for free. It's good for a whole year, and you don't have to buy it ahead of time. Just buy it in the first place on the list that you see.

If you want to get the most out of your card, come back in less than a year to visit the places you missed.

7. Have a big breakfast and a small lunch.

During your trip to Ireland, you should eat your hot breakfast, even if you usually have "just a black coffee" in the morning. From the fanciest hotel to the smallest B&B, everyone takes pride in serving a great breakfast. There will be a lot of choices, and a full breakfast will get you ready for the day.

Now you only need a small lunch, so go to a nice café and get soup. You can get a big bowl of homemade soup with a chunky piece of good bread almost anywhere for a very fair price. It will taste great and fill you up.

If the weather is nice, you could also go to the store and buy some fruit, crackers or bread rolls, and a nice piece of local cheese. Then, have a lunch somewhere nice.

8. Eat dinner early

Almost all restaurants offer great deals to people who order their food before 7 p.m. (though this can be as early as 6:30 p.m. in some places). Most of the time, these are two or three items from a special menu that cost a lot less than dinner, especially at fancier restaurants.

Even though you won't have as many options as when you eat à la carte, the food and cooking will still be of a high standard, and you'll save a lot of money.

9. Try to find deals

You might use sites like Groupon to find deals back home. If you plan, you can also use these while you're in Ireland.

A lot of places offer discounts to seniors, students, and kids, so make sure you ask for them if you are one of those groups.

Ask for a group discount if you are four or more people going on private trips, ferries, or activities like golf, water sports, or other similar things. They are always there; tour operators regularly receive them, and there's no reason they shouldn't also be given to you. You should get a discount of 10% to 20%.

10. Get on board with the tax refund plan

Yes, it's a bit complicated and you need to be very organized with your paperwork, but almost everything you buy in Ireland is subject to sales tax, or VAT, of 21%. If you are not from the EU, you can get that money back in full. Anyone who buys something will save one-fifth of the price, so don't miss this chance.

GALWAY Insider Tips

➢ **Festivals – all the time**

People in Galway love to party and always seem to be going from one event to the next. As a joint city of culture, it has a huge schedule of events, on top of the festivals that are already going on. The word "Cúirt" comes from the Old Irish language and means "court of poetry." It is also the name of a literature event that runs from April 20th to April 25th and has had authors like Seamus Heaney, Edna O'Brien, and Allen Ginsberg. Galway Arts Festival in July (13–26) seems like it would be fun for everyone in the city. Children can get ideas from the Baboró event. The Galway Races aren't just about the horses, and our Oyster event (25–27 September) celebrates a local treat.

➢ **Two walks from Wolfe Tone Bridge**

From Wolfe Tone Bridge, you can go on two very different walks. First, go south past the Claddagh area and along Nimmo's Pier and the beach until you see the Promenade on your right. It was built in the middle of the 1800s and has been added to over time. People who walk, jog, stroll, crawl, and more come here to enjoy the sea air and the way the light and colors change in Galway Bay. One of the best things about Galway, it's about three miles long.

The second path goes north along the canal to University College. It enters the grounds through the front gate and turns right at Bailey Allen Hall to reach the river. For a couple of miles, follow the stream to get to Dangan, which is on the other side of the ruins of Menlo Castle. You get a different picture of Galway from this, but the Prom is the one for me because I grew up by the sea.

➢ **Great pubs**

People who like whiskey go to either Garavan's on William Street or Sonny Molloy's on High Street, which both have a huge selection of names to try. Great gins can be found at Freeney's, which is also on High Street, the Hyde Bar, which is on Forster Street, and Tigh Nora, which is on Cross Street. Folk music is what bars are all about, and the Crane Bar on Sea Road is the place for true fans. If you want to feel the vibe of the streets, grab a drink outside of Tigh Neachtain, another classic bar, and watch the world go by. I've been to all of these places, but since I'm old and gray and like good pub talk, I'd suggest the Bunch of Grapes on High Street and Lonergans in Salthill (no websites). Micil, a small distillery, is now making poitín in the Oslo Bar in Salthill. It's open Tuesday through Saturday at 2 p.m., 4 p.m., and 6 p.m. for tours and tastes.

➤ Happy theater sparks the mind

This word comes from Old Irish and means "the energy of a young calf leaping around the meadow in the spring." It's also the name of a theater company in Galway that puts on shows outside. A Macnas parade is a wild party full of creativity, color, energy, music, fire, dance, and chaos. Most people in Galway feel carefree during these events; it's like a spell spreads through the city and makes everyone happy for the day. Its plans for 2020 are based on the tale of Gilgamesh. Events 10-12 April, 21 June, 19-28 November, 12 December,

➤ Seafood and views of the sea

If you want to taste Galway, you have to start with its famous oysters, which you can get when there's an R in the month. Pacific oysters aren't as good as the ones we get here in Ireland. My favorites are from Cooke's restaurant on Abbeygate Street and Kasbah, a wine bar next to its parent pub Tigh Neachtain. Galwegians have been going to Colleran's butcher shop since 1935, and their black pudding is also a local favorite. On Churchyard Street, Sheridan's Cheesemongers is a must-see for anyone interested in Irish, local, or foreign cheese.

With views of both the river and the sea, Ard Bia by the Spanish Arch is a great place to eat and enjoy the scenery.

From the waterside location of Corrib House Tea Rooms, you can see beautiful views.

The tea rooms serve a wide range of teas and offer bed and breakfast (doubles from €120). The tuck shop next door to the school, Kai on Sea Road, used to be there. Now it's a restaurant that focuses on organic and wild regional foods.

➤ The Collegiate Church of St. Nicholas

This church was built in 1320, which means it is 700 years old this year, which is a great birthday present. It's a must-see because it shows a small part of the history of the city: it was built by the Knights Templar with help from the 14 most important merchant families in Galway, and over the years Christopher Columbus, Oliver Cromwell's troops, lepers, famine victims, and many worshipers have all been there. People from both Catholic and Protestant groups have lived in and run it. It is now owned by the Church of Ireland, but it is truly an inclusive building. There's a busy market outside every Saturday.

St. Nicholas's.ie

➤ A labyrinth of books

Find Charlie Bryne's Bookshop on Middle Street if you like your independent bookstores to be a creepy maze of rooms. It's like a maze with more than 100,000 books—new, used, and old—but the staff knows their way around, so they can help you find your way. It's not a wonder that it won Irish Bookstore of the Year in 2019. Just like at my place, Kennys, you might run into a visiting author there. The Bell Book and Candle in the Small Crane Square is a fun place to visit with a wide range of books, comics, music, and pictures.

➤ Explore the poetry walk in Galway.

There are more than 20 songs and other pieces of writing about Galway on plaques all over the city. Together with Galway City Council, the store I help run puts it together, and each bronze or stone plaque is in a place that fits with what it says. There are poems by James Joyce, Seamus Heaney, Moya Cannon, Máire Holmes, Roger McGough, and others. Each one offers a moment of peace to help people in cities feel better. Find them and enjoy a pleasant treat.

You can find out more at Kenny. ie, and you can get a trail map at the Galway tourist office on Forster Street.

➢ A sporting event... with sticks

With 34,000 seats, the Pearse Stadium in Salthill is the perfect place to see the exciting and particularly Irish sports of hurling and Gaelic football. It's very hard to play badly because you need to be very skilled and have great hand-eye coordination to throw. The sticks look like weapons, but they're rarely used that way. If you like rugby, Connacht Rugby plays at the Sportsground on College Road, which is only a five-minute walk from the city center. For the best vibe, try to find a spot on the Clan Terrace.

➢ Irish Galway GAA

The Story Behind the Claddagh Ring

The Claddagh was a fishing village on the Corrib River, right where it meets the sea. It had cobblestone streets, mud-walled homes, and a strong sense of independence, with its own rules and king. In the late 1920s, doctors said it was dangerous, so it was torn down and concrete houses were built in its place. The village had its own type of wedding ring, which was passed down from mother to daughter. When you're single, you wear it with the crown facing the knuckle. When you get married, you wear it with the crown facing the nail.

African pirates are said to have kidnapped Galway man Richard Joyce and sold him as a slave to a Moorish goldsmith who taught him how to make jewelry. He was set free in 1689 and went back to Galway to start his own business. He is thought to have made some of the first known Claddagh rings.

GALWAY Cultural Tips

Galway is a place with a lot of history and culture. When you go, here are some cultural tips to keep in mind:

Do not abuse the Irish language. Irish is one of Ireland's two national languages, and many people in Galway speak it. Simple Irish words like "hello" (Dia dhuit), "goodbye" (Slán), and "please" (Le do thoil) are good to learn if you can.

You should know about Irish habits and customs. For example, 15-20% of the bill is what most people leave as a tip for waiters and waitresses. People also think it's rude to talk on the phone in public places like bars and restaurants.

Have fun with the music and the dance. People know Galway for its lively dance and music scene. You can hear live traditional Irish music in a lot of pubs and clubs in the city. Throughout the city, you can also see traditional Irish dancing shows everywhere.

Go to the market in Galway. You can buy fresh food, crafts, and other things at the Galway Market once a week. You can learn about Galway's history and meet people from the area.

Go to a fair. Events like the Galway Arts Festival, the Galway International Oyster Festival, and the Galway Film Fleadh happen all year long in Galway. Going to these events is a fun way to learn about Galway's culture and meet people from around the world.

Put on the right clothes. Make sure you dress appropriately when you go to religious places like churches and cathedrals. This means that your knees and hips should be covered.

Pay attention to how loud you are. Galway isn't a very noisy city, but be aware of your noise level, especially at night.

Take care of the earth. Galway is a lovely city that has a lot of beautiful nature areas nearby. Be careful not to leave any signs behind when you hike or explore the area.

CHAPTER NINE

10 Best Day Trips from GALWAY (By a Local!)

People from all over the world love to visit Galway, which is on the west side of Ireland. The city is handy for day trips around the Galway area, as well as having interesting history, shops, and pubs.

This section of this guide has 10 of the best day trips from Galway. You can choose from popular destinations like the Cliffs of Moher or more unique places like the Burren.

Ten of the best day trips you can take from Galway

As part of this 10-day Ireland road trip plan in June, I visited the Galway area. I stayed in Galway for two nights and then went to see well-known places like the Cliffs of Moher, the Burren, Kylemore Abbey, and the Connemara.

Galway is one of a few towns in Ireland that makes a great base to see the Irish countryside if you'd rather stay in one place longer than drive from one place to another. You don't have to pack up every night to go to a new hotel when you leave Galway. YOU can plan many day trips.

Are you ready to see more of Galway? Come on!

1. Cliffs of Moher

Cliffs of Moher Ireland

There is no doubt that a walk of the Cliffs of Moher from Galway is the most popular thing to do in Ireland and close to Galway.

Along the Atlantic Ocean, the Cliffs of Moher are about 5 miles long and get up to 700 feet high in some places. From either side of the path that goes out from the visitor center, you can see beautiful views for miles.

But the Cliffs of Moher's unique natural beauty comes from the way they are laid out, which looks like an accordion. After a while, you can see more of the rocks, and if you're lucky, the sun will shine on them just right. You really can't miss them when you go to Ireland!

Ways to Get There:

It takes about an hour and twenty minutes to drive from Galway to the Cliffs of Moher.

You could spend all day at the Cliffs of Moher if you walk a lot or all of the coastal roads between Hags Head and Doolin, but most people only stay for a few hours, either in the morning or afternoon. This means that you can go to other places on a full-day trip.

You could easily spend some time in the Burren, go to the town of Doolin, or stop at the castles of Doonagore and Dunguiare.

Tours of the Cliffs of Moher by bus from Galway

You can also take a day trip by bus from Galway to the Cliffs of Moher if you don't have a car. Because every tour is a little different, you should read about what each one includes before you book.

This well-known Cliffs of Moher tour goes to Dunguaire Castle, then drives through the Burren and stops at Corcomroe Abbey. Finally, it spends two hours at the Cliffs of Moher. After that, you'll take pictures at Doolin Pier and then go to the town of Doolin on your own for lunch. For an extra cost, you can also add a Cliffs of Moher tour to your day.

If you don't have much time, this half-day trip from Galway to the Cliffs of Moher lets you spend two hours at the Cliffs before going back to the city.

You can also go on a trip called Cliffs of Moher Explorer which gives you time to walk along the cliff path from Doolin to the Cliffs of Moher.

This Cliffs of Moher tour only goes to the Cliffs and the town of Doolin, which is close by. Going to see the sights will be more relaxing because of the later start time.

2. Aran Islands

On the Irish island of Aran, Inishmore

The Aran Islands are made up of three islands: Inis Mor, Inis Meain, and Inis Oirr. They are all close to the port of Galway. There is a lot of natural beauty, old-world culture, and history on these islands.

People in the area speak Irish as their first language, but don't worry—English is still spoken by many. The islands have historical places that go back to the Stone Age. These include the Round Tower, the Seven Churches, and Dun Aengus, a stone fort from the 1500s B.C.

Bikes can be rented to get around the islands. Along the way, you can enjoy the views of the coast, visit many Celtic and Early Christian sites, and see long stretches of stone walls that shape the scenery.

Ways to Get There:

Every day of the year, boats go to the islands from Rossaveal, which is just outside of Galway. From March to October, they go from Doolin. You can choose to stay on one island or go to all of them.

Trip to the Aran Islands in one day from Galway

You can also take trips from Galway if you don't have a car and want to get to the ferry.

This day trip from Galway to the Aran Islands gives you two hours to explore Inis Oirr, which is the smallest of the Aran Islands. After that, you'll have an hour to enjoy the Cliffs of Moher's views.

This trip from Galway to the Aran Islands lasts for 4 1/2 hours on Inis Mor. The boat ride back along the Cliffs of Moher lets you see how big they are from the Atlantic Ocean.

On a different day trip from Galway to the Aran Islands, you can cruise along the Cliffs of Moher and spend two hours on Inis Oirr instead.

3. Connemara

Connemara National Park Ireland

Just an hour's drive north and west of Galway City is the rocky beauty of the Connemara. Mountains, valleys, lakes, and harbors in the area fit together like puzzle parts to make a beautiful view that changes from soft yellows in the spring to oranges and reds in the fall. The colors made me think of the beautiful roads in County Wicklow.

Kylemore Abbey and the Connemara National Park are two well-known places in the Connemara. But if you drive along its beautiful routes, you'll see castles, lookouts along the Wild Atlantic Way, beaches with turquoise water, colorful seaside towns, and lots of sheep!

Ways to Get There:

From Galway, N59 takes you to the Connemara and then to the Connemara Loop, a beautiful road that goes around the area for 50 miles. The drive from Galway to Kylemore Abbey is about 75 minutes if you go straight there.

Tour of Connemara from Galway

A lot of people who visit this part of Ireland like to take day trips to Connemara from Galway. You can still enjoy this beautiful part of the Irish countryside even if you don't have a car.

You will see a lot of what Connemara has to offer on this trip. Go to Killary Fjord and the town of Leenane, which is on the water. Get some rest at Kylemore Abbey and take in the beautiful mountain and beach views in the area.

Take this day trip from Galway to Connemara National Park and stay there all day. You'll stop for pictures all over the Connemara on your way to and from the national park. You can walk for a few hours at the national park.

4. Wild Atlantic Way

Road Connemara Ireland

The Wild Atlantic Way is a long, beautiful seaside path that goes from the southern coast of Ireland, near Cork, to the northern tip of the country, in Derry. It goes along 1,600 miles of the Atlantic coast and farmland in Ireland.

Most tourists drive parts of this road, and luckily, the route is easy to split up into different drives based on where you are in Ireland.

Ways to Get There:

You can drive from Galway to Clifden and then onto the Sky Road Loop in the Connemara. Along the way, you can see Dog's Bay, the Twelve Bens, and Clifden Castle. On a different part of the road, you can go from Clifden to Westport and see places like Killary Harbor, Connemara National Park, and Kylemore Abbey.

You might also want to drive south of Galway. Along the Wild Atlantic Way are also the Cliffs of Moher, Doolin, and The Burren.

Tours of the Wild Atlantic Way from Galway:

Along the Wild Atlantic Way, this day trip goes through towns by the sea and into the Connemara. You'll also have three hours to look around Connemara National Park and enjoy the ocean views from the Sky Road Loop.

5. Castles Near Galway

Connemara Aughnanure Castle Ireland

Irish buildings are something you can't see enough of. Whether they are beautifully renovated or falling apart, Ireland's countryside is full of castles.

It's easy to plan a day of castle exploring if you live in Galway or are close to it. Some of the most well-known castles close to Galway are Aughnanure, Ballynahinch, Clifden, Doonagore, Dunguaire, Bunratty, King John's, and Ashford.

Ways to Get There:

If you have any other Galway day tours planned, you might get to see some of these houses as part of those. Then, make a plan for how to get to the other castles you want to see.

Among other things, Aughnanure, Ballynahinch, Clifden, and other stops in Connemara can be put together. Both Bunratty Castle and King John's Castle are close to or in Limerick, and it's easy to see both in one day.

Dublin to Castle Day Tours:

This tour from Galway takes you to see castles, learn about history, and see beautiful buildings. There is time at Kylemore Abbey and stops at Aughnanure, Ballynahinch, and Clifden castles.

6. The Burren

Stone Age Tomb The Burren Ireland

It is part of a UNESCO World Heritage Site, along with the Cliffs of Moher. The Burren's limestone scenery takes you to another world and back to the Stone Age at the same time.

There are stone forts and Neolithic tombs here, as well as a unique biome. You can walk through Burren National Park to enjoy the beautiful scenery and learn about the trees, animals, and Stone Age people that still live here.

There's also the beautiful and creepy Corcomroe Abbey, which has been abandoned and is a sign of the more recent Middle Ages.

You can see both the Burren and the Cliffs of Moher at the same time. You could spend a day "getting lost" in the Burren's past, small villages, and culture, though.

Ways to Get There:

It only takes 45 minutes to drive from Galway to Corcomroe Abbey, which is at the northern end of the Burren. I can get to Burren National Park in an hour by car.

Day trips to the Burren from Galway:

Going on a walk with a group is the best way to see the Burren without a car. A lot of the time, these tours include time at both the Cliffs of Moher and the Burren.

The Burren and the Cliffs of Moher are both on this trip. The Stone Age tombs of Gleninsheen Wedge Tomb and the Poulnabrone Dolmen are two of the most interesting places to visit in the Burren.

A cool natural feature of the Burren is its network of caves. This tour goes into Aillwee Cave, which is one of the most well-known in the area, and then ends at the Cliffs of Moher.

7. Bunratty Castle

Bunratty Castle Ireland

You might not need a whole day to see Bunratty Castle, but you could spend a few hours walking around the castle and the town of old Irish homes to learn more about the area and the types of people who lived there.

Bunratty Castle is also known for being a great place for families. For families with young children, this could be a fun way to learn about Ireland's history in a real and hands-on way.

You could also spend half a day in the Burren or go to nearby Limerick or Ennis if you had a full day. In either case, you should buy your Bunratty Castle tickets ahead of time to skip the line.

Ways to Get There:

Gaol is only an hour's drive south of Bunratty Castle. So you know what to expect, you will go through the Burren and east of the Cliffs of Moher.

A day trip from Galway to Bunratty Castle:

There aren't any group trips from Galway that go to Bunratty Castle that let you spend time there, which is too bad.

8. Dog's Bay Beach

Connemara Dogs Bay Beach Ireland

During some times of the year, you might be able to spend a day at the beach in Ireland! I have to say that Ireland's beaches were one of the best parts of my trip. I had no idea that the water would be that color. Like the Caribbean!

Don't go from Galway to any other beach because Dog's Bay Beach is the most beautiful. Another great place to put your toes in the sand is Gurteen Beach, which is close by.

Both beaches have soft white sand and are in coves, which means the water is quieter than at beaches that face the open ocean.

Ways to Get There:

You can get to both beaches by car in about 75 minutes from Galway. It's possible to spend half a day in each place because you'll be going to and from the Connemara.

You'll need a car to get to Dog's Bay and Gurteen Beaches, but not to the other places on this list.

9. Cong

Cong Abbey Ireland

The village of Cong is north of Galway. It has a long history and became famous when the romantic comedy "The Quiet Man" was shot there in 1952.

John Wayne and Maureen O'Hara were in the movie. The movie has its own small museum and a statue.

Cong has a lot of past as well. Old Cong Abbey ruins can be seen in the village. They were built in the 1100s. This is where the Cong Cross was found. It is now on show in Dublin. It's thought to have been made around the year 1100.

At Cong, you can also go to Ashford Castle, which is only a short drive away. There are no castle tours because the castle is a hotel. But people can enjoy the grounds and events, and they can even make lunch reservations to get a look inside.

Ways to Get There:

Galway takes 40 minutes to get to Cong. If you plan your day well, you might be able to spend some time in the Cong area and then go back through part of the Connemara on your way back to Galway.

For day trips from Galway to Cong:

On this full-day tour, you can see both Cong and the Connemara. Some of the sights are the famous Kylemore Abbey and the Cong Abbey, which was built in the 1100s.

10. The castle of Dunguaire

Castle Dunguaire in Ireland

Early in the 1500s, Dunguaire Castle was built. The castle looks like a tower house and is set in a beautiful spot on the shore of Galway Bay. This building is one of the most photographed in all of Ireland.

The castle and protective walls have been fixed up to look like they did in the 1600s. You can tour the castle or go to a castle dinner to enjoy the atmosphere of the castle at night.

Ways to Get There:

It only takes 30 minutes to drive from Galway to Dunguaire Castle. Since the castle is just south of the city, you can also visit the Cliffs of Moher or go on an adventure in the Burren at the same time.

There aren't any day tours that just go to Dunguaire Castle, but this one stops there so people can see the outside of the castle before going to the Cliffs of Moher and then the Burren.

CHAPTER TEN

7 DAYS IN GALWAY: The Perfect GALWAY Itinerary for First-Time Visitors

Day 1:

- Arrive in Galway City and check into your hotel.

- Take a walk around the city center and visit some of the main attractions, such as the Spanish Arch, the Claddagh Ring, and the Galway Cathedral.

- Have dinner at one of Galway's many excellent restaurants, such as The Quay House or McDonagh's.

Day 2:

- Take a day trip to the Aran Islands. These three islands are located just off the coast of Galway and offer a unique glimpse into traditional Irish culture.

- Visit the island of Inis Mór, the largest of the three islands, and see the Dún Aonghasa cliff fort.

- Take a walk along the Worm's Head, a natural rock formation that resembles a worm.

- Have dinner at one of the many restaurants on Inis Mór.

- Visit the Connemara National Park, a beautiful park with stunning scenery.

- Hike to Diamond Hill, a mountain that offers panoramic views of the park.

- Visit Kylemore Abbey, a Benedictine abbey that is now a hotel and visitor attraction.

- Have dinner at one of the many restaurants in the village of Clifden.

- Take a boat trip to the Cliffs of Moher, one of Ireland's most iconic natural attractions.

- Walk along the cliffs and enjoy the stunning views.

- Visit the O'Brien's Tower, a 19th-century tower that offers panoramic views of the cliffs.

- Have dinner at one of the many restaurants in the village of Doolin.

- Visit the Galway City Museum to learn about the history of Galway and the surrounding area.

- Visit the Galway Cathedral, a beautiful neo-Gothic cathedral.

- Take a walk through Claddagh, Galway's oldest neighborhood.

- Have dinner at one of the many restaurants in the Claddagh.

Day 6:

- Visit the Galway Market, a weekly market where you can buy fresh produce, crafts, and other goods.

- Visit the Galway Cathedral Coffee Shop for a cup of coffee and a slice of cake.

- Take a walk along the River Corrib.

- Have dinner at one of the many restaurants along the river.

Day 7:

- Depart from Galway City.

This is just a suggested itinerary by NOMAD NICK, and you can customize it to fit your interests and budget.

For example, if you are interested in history, you could spend more time visiting historical sites such as the Galway City Museum and the Galway Cathedral.

If you are interested in nature, you could spend more time exploring the Connemara National Park and the Cliffs of Moher.

And if you are on a tight budget, you could eat at less expensive restaurants and stay in hostels or guesthouses.

No matter what you choose to do, you are sure to have a wonderful time in Galway. It is a beautiful city with a lot to offer visitors.

CHAPTER ELEVEN

GALWAY Travel Tips and Tricks from a Local (for 2024)

If you're planning a trip to Galway in 2024, you're in for a treat. Galway, often referred to as the "City of Tribes," is a vibrant and culturally rich destination on the west coast of Ireland. As a seasoned traveler and local enthusiast, I'm here to share some valuable tips and tricks to make your Galway experience unforgettable.

1. Explore the Heart of Galway City:
- Begin your adventure in Eyre Square, a bustling hub surrounded by shops, cafes, and green spaces. It's the perfect place to get your bearings and soak up some local atmosphere.
- Stroll along Shop Street, a pedestrian-friendly street brimming with street performers, boutiques, and traditional Irish pubs.

2. Savor Galway's Culinary Delights:
- Galway is a food lover's paradise. Try fresh seafood dishes at local restaurants like McDonagh's, where fish and chips are a must.
- Don't miss a taste of traditional Irish stews, made with hearty ingredients like lamb, potatoes, and carrots.

3. Witness Cultural Wonders:
- Immerse yourself in Galway's rich cultural scene. Check out live music sessions in pubs like Tig

Coili, where traditional Irish tunes will serenade you.

- Visit the Galway City Museum for a fascinating journey through the city's history and heritage.

4. Attend Festivals and Events:

- Galway is famous for its festivals. Depending on your travel dates, you might catch the Galway International Arts Festival or the Galway Oyster Festival, both offering unique experiences.

5. Explore the Natural Beauty:

- Take a day trip to the stunning Cliffs of Moher, located just a short drive from Galway. The breathtaking views of the Atlantic Ocean are worth the journey.
- Discover the picturesque landscapes of Connemara, with its rugged mountains, lakes, and charming villages.

6. Transportation Made Easy:

- Getting around Galway is a breeze. The city center is compact and walkable, making it convenient for exploring on foot.
- If you plan to explore the wider region, consider renting a car for flexibility, especially if you want to venture into the scenic countryside.

7. Choose Accommodation Wisely:

- Galway offers a range of accommodation options, from cozy B&Bs to boutique hotels. Be sure to book your stay well in advance, especially during peak tourist seasons.

8. Connect with Locals:
- Strike up conversations with friendly locals. They'll gladly share their favorite hidden gems and insider tips for an authentic Galway experience.

9. Embrace the Language:
- While English is widely spoken, you might encounter signs and place names in Irish (Gaeilge). Learn a few basic Irish words like "Dia dhuit" (hello) and "Sláinte" (cheers) to connect with the locals.

10. Capture the Memories:
- Don't forget your camera! Galway offers countless Instagram-worthy moments, from colorful storefronts to breathtaking landscapes. Be ready to capture the magic.

11. Plan for the Weather:
- Irish weather can be unpredictable. Pack layers and a waterproof jacket to stay comfortable in rain or shine.

12. Respect Local Customs:
- Lastly, be mindful of local customs and traditions. Avoid stereotypes, and instead, engage with the culture respectfully.

Galway is a place where old traditions meet modern vibrancy, creating a truly unique travel experience. With these tips in hand, you're ready to embark on a memorable journey through this captivating city and its surrounding wonders. Safe travels, explorers!

FINAL THOUGHT BY NOMAD NICK

Galway is a city with something to offer everyone. Whether you're interested in history, culture, food, nightlife, or nature, you're sure to find something to your liking in Galway.

I hope this travel guide has inspired you to visit Galway and experience all that this amazing city has to offer. I encourage you to explore the city's rich history, vibrant culture, and delicious food. Be sure to catch a traditional Irish music session in one of the many pubs, and take a day trip to one of the beautiful beaches or islands in the surrounding area.

Galway is a city that will stay with you long after you leave. It's a city with a warm and welcoming atmosphere, and it's a city that's full of life. I can't wait to see you in Galway soon!

ALWAYS REMEMBER THIS TIPS AS WE HAVE DISCUSSED THEM ABOVE

- Galway is a very walkable city, so be sure to pack comfortable shoes.

- If you're planning on visiting during the summer months, be sure to book your accommodation in advance, as Galway can get very busy.

- Galway is a relatively small city, but it can still be easy to get lost. Be sure to pick up a map of the city from the tourist office.

- Galway is a very safe city, but it's always a good idea to be aware of your surroundings and take precautions against petty theft.

- Be sure to try some of Galway's famous seafood, such as oysters, mussels, and salmon.

- Galway is a very friendly city, so don't be afraid to ask for help or directions if you need them.

I hope you enjoyed reading my Galway travel guide! If you did, I would be grateful if you would leave a review on Amazon or at your favorite bookstore. Your review will help other travelers find my guide and plan their trip to Galway.

I also encourage you to visit my Amazon author page HERE OR visit amzn.to/48OKIpw to browse my other travel guides. I have written guides to a variety of destinations, including Ireland, Italy, Germany, and France. I am also constantly working on new guides, so be sure to check back often for updates.

Thank you for your support! I hope to see you on my next adventure!

NOMAD NICK!

Printed in Great Britain
by Amazon